Paradox for Life Review

Paradox for Life Review

A Guide for Enhancing Older Adults' Self-Esteem

James J. Magee, PhD

JASON ARONSON
Lanham • Boulder • New York • Toronto • Plymouth, UK

PROPERTY OF W...
SOCIAL WOR... ...RARY
DISCARD

Published by Jason Aronson
A wholly owned subsidiary of The Rowman & Littlefield Publishing Group, Inc.
4501 Forbes Boulevard, Suite 200, Lanham, Maryland 20706
www.rowmanlittlefield.com

Estover Road, Plymouth PL6 7PY, United Kingdom

British Library Cataloguing in Publication Information Available

Library of Congress Cataloging-in-Publication Data

Magee, James J. (James Joseph)
Paradox for life review : a guide for enhancing older adults' self-esteem / James J. Magee.
p. cm.
Includes bibliographical references and index.
ISBN 978-0-7657-0867-0 (hbk. : alk. paper)
1. Older people—Psychology. 2. Reminiscing in old age. 3. Self-esteem in old age. I. Title.
BF724.85.R45M33 2012
155.67'19—dc23
2011037564

Printed in the United States of America

For my cousin Helen and her husband George Henry,
who took me in when my parents died
and
for my sister Elizabeth and her husband John Horan,
best of friends to each other and to me

Contents

Acknowledgments

Among this book's many parents are Dr. Charles Fahey, founding director of Fordham University's Third Age Center, who introduced me to the personal and societal resources that protect the self-esteem of older adults. Another is Dr. Philip Guerin, founding director of The Center for Family Learning, who taught me how to assess the functioning of extended family systems and to help family members reframe their experiences through paradox.

The College of New Rochelle provided me with faculty development grants to organize the content of this book and a sabbatical leave to complete writing it. My colleagues at Gill Library generously facilitated my access to a range of sources. Dr. Kenneth Doka, my esteemed colleague in Gerontology, made recommendations that considerably enhanced the quality of the manuscript. I am especially grateful to my wife Nancy for her patience, her computer expertise, and her linguistic precision. Above all, I am beholden to my fellow older adults who have graciously shared their life review with me.

Introduction

This book is a companion for older adults as they review their lives. Drawing on findings from the social sciences and forty-two examples of life review, it explains the benefits of reminiscing in general and the advantages of life review groups in particular. Its special focus is showing how group members can access a variety of paradoxes that promote self-esteem by integrating their personal history with a sense of purpose for the future.

The book is a guide for confidants and group facilitators who can use its interdisciplinary knowledge base to help older adults find meaning and self-acceptance in their life reviewed. It shows how three perspectives on personal development each affect the level of self-esteem, that lens through which older adults review their reminiscences. It prepares facilitators to introduce group members to paradoxes from lyrics and drama, Eastern and Western mystical traditions, varieties of word play, intergenerational family dynamics and poetry. These paradoxes then become new lenses through which older adults can look upon their personal history with compassion and wisdom.

The book is a resource for family caretakers who can enrich reviewers' memories and their own attentiveness to them. It shows how caretakers can use paradoxes to augment reminiscences, especially those in which they have been participants. Self-interest in a reviewer's accounts of family history may take kin further than altruism may reach when listening to family folklore.

The book is a manual for mental health professionals and students preparing for careers in gerontology, nursing, pastoral counseling, psychology and social work. These professionals will discover how using paradoxes can evoke within themselves empathic responses to the memories older adults share with them.

All parties will recognize in William Faulkner's aphorism a characteristic inherent in reminiscing: its plasticity. Long term memories are creative reconstructions rather than objective, photographic images of past events. Thus, a cluster of age related stressors—retirement, primary care giving, widowhood, illness, dependence—can so belabor the vigorous self-esteem of some, and overwhelm the meager self-esteem of others, that older adults may recall a personal history replete with repeated failures and disappointments. Fortunately, this pliability also means that older adults can use resources at hand to function at the optimal limit their self-esteem allows, and view memories through a lens of compassion for self and others. Such a lens does not excuse the past recalled, but its widened perspective reveals the multivalent influences ever present in human activity.

LIFE REVIEW GROUPS

Chapter 1 explains the processes of reminiscing and life review, particularly in groups. Reminiscing evokes long term memories that revive the joys of relationships and the consolations of reconciliations. The memories both draw on older adults' reservoirs of entertaining tales, and recover problem-solving precedents relevant to issues they are now confronting. Life review is a form of reminiscence that focuses on assessing the life remembered according to reviewers' current values. Its goal is enabling older adults to own their personal history in an acceptance of themselves as good enough.

The chapter shows how life review groups become a resource for all their members, even those with encumbered self-esteem. The character of the groups themselves, intentionally educational and open to all, is itself beneficial. Their announced purpose facilitates self-disclosure, and similarities that invariably appear among reminiscences prompt further candid recollections from participants. Group members responding with empathy rather than judgment demonstrate how self-disclosure is a gift that benefits everyone. Members discover that it is safe to expect for themselves the same attentive respect with which they have responded to others.

The social dimensions of sharing memories with a group provide further resources when older adults' "cope runneth over." Fellowship allows older adults to glean advice without appearing vulnerable, to access shared referral services, or to find a colleague ready to perform some favor which they can return. It is not surprising that older men who reminisce are found to be less depressed than those who do not.

THE "SELF" IN SELF-ESTEEM

Chapter 2 explores the *epigenetic self* which evolves over a lifetime by integrating a sequence of maturational selves. Ideally during this integration the current maturational self subsumes the competencies from preceding selves, and draws upon resources in the environment to express newly formed knowledge and skills. Children internalize the earliest maturational self, the *observant-self,* by identifying with the attitudes of parents, kin, and significant others. When caretakers' expectations are appropriate and conveyed empathically, they further children's sense of self-esteem.

In a healthy scenario, maturation then moves adolescents to the *want-to-be-self,* that "perfect" self they wish to become. After age twenty-five or so, maturation moves young adults to integrate these earlier selves within a *competent-self.* This self empowers the transitions of young adults to employment, to a residence of their own, and to an informed decision to enter into marriage or a committed relationship. Maturation next moves mature adults toward an *inclusive-self* with an ever widening awareness of everyone's lifelong interdependence upon each other. This self motivates mature adults to altruistic efforts that assuage suffering, further social justice, and benefit future generations.

Chapter 3 examines the family scripted self. Families perpetuate their identity when older generations assign younger members "scripts" for parts in the long running family drama. The integrity of the drama then weighs upon members to remain in character as they play out the family's recurrent issues. Members can elaborate upon their parts, enter and withdraw from the stage on their own initiative, and improvise their lines so long as they remain true to their character and provide one another with the cues they need to play upon the family stage. Family identity, individual scripts, and ongoing issues are inseparably entwined.

Chapter 4 elaborates upon a spiritual, *metaphysical self,* a universal source of unconditional acceptance and an unfathomable wellspring sustaining existence-as-gift. Depending on people's perspectives, the metaphysical self may refer to their connectedness to their life force, or to their self as rooted in an Absolute whose antecedent and abiding regard grounds the personal self. Thus, self-esteem proceeds from grasping, in Paul Tillich's phrase, that "you are accepted, accepted by that which is greater than you."[2]

SELF-ESTEEM AND SHAME

Chapter 5 progresses from examining the self reviewed to exploring the self-esteem of the reviewers. For self-esteem, the abiding judgment individuals make about their competence and worth, is the lens through which they review their personal history, discern meaning in their lives, and decide whether they are "good enough." Older adults with vigorous self-esteem see themselves as capable, significant, and intrinsically good enough to allow the life reviewed to replenish the life at hand. They scan and assess their past from the perspective of an inner-directed, interdependent self, and accept the maturational selves their memories reveal to them. They can observe and assess themselves with realism and compassion.

Self-esteem, of course, exists along a continuum, and a person's location on the continuum remains basically unaltered, unless there is a clinical intervention. Nonetheless, life review groups using paradoxes can increase the frequency and duration in the times their members function at the optimal limit their self-esteem allows. Paradoxes have enabled reviewers to "play at the top of their game."

Chapter 6 addresses the shame embedded at the other end of the self-esteem continuum. Its ultimate expression occurs when toxic scripts and triangles fuse shame and identity in children, estrange adults from their very self, and ensure that reminiscences will focus disproportionately upon deeply felt personal inadequacies. Toxic issues, recurring over generations whenever scripts prompt family members to react with excruciating anxiety, transmit these scripts to children through triangles that form when members feel that an issue threatens the relationship between them. Quarreling parents, for instance, may draw in a child to stabilize their original twosome. Paradoxes have been able to penetrate this toxicity and open these triangles.

PARADOXES FOR PROTECTING SELF-ESTEEM

Chapter 7 explains how paradoxes work, and shows how group members can stretch their self-esteem by drawing upon a variety of accessible paradoxes. Facilitators introduce paradoxes to their groups as catalysts for revealing engrossing and instructive reminiscences. Paradoxes are self-contradictory statements or events that initially arrest the attention of reviewers, but for those who can stay with the tension of holding opposites simultaneously, they can evoke syntheses that transcend the contradictions. These syntheses, in turn, modify the shaming lens which had been distorting their memories. Paradoxes, for example, have enabled reviewers to recognize how the formative components of their identity lie in the very relationships that transmitted shame. For these reviewers, their shame-inducing history became a quixotic component of self-acceptance.

Chapter 8 records how members of life review groups use *poetic paradoxes* to transcend their recall of troubled memories. They select from anthologies that facilitators provide the poems that express themes which have been prominent in their own lives, and which incorporate a paradoxical point of view about these themes. Members may also choose such poems from the works of their favorite bard or from poems providing paradoxes about a treasured subject, such as nature's beauty, marital and parental ties, or perseverance in adversity. Others with few literary associations have found helpful imagery in the lyrics of songs and family jingles.

Chapter 9 explores the identical process reviewers follow in converting two kinds of *word-play* into paradoxes: metaphors in lyrics and homonyms in the reviewers' own speech. Metaphors are comparisons that communicate insights by transferring the literal meaning of a word to a different category with which it shares certain characteristics, e.g., "When I finally stood up to that bully, I felt bold as a lion."

This metaphor becomes paradoxical once a facilitator or colleague asks, "What other characteristics of a lion besides 'boldness' could appear in your reminiscences?" The question challenges the reviewer by proposing that *unintended* characteristics of the object referred to (the lion) can be the key in opening new perspectives about themes and scenes under review. The reviewer's staying power in following the free association after that exchange evokes the recognition, the "aha!" experience, of new insight into memories. Free association, of course, does not occur randomly. Psychological openness summons the wants, fears, and goals that over-determine the emergent content of thought.

Homonyms here includes both homophones that sound alike but differ in spelling and meaning and homonyms that are spelled and pronounced alike but differ in meaning. Group facilitators point out homonyms that appear in members' comments, and distribute books with lists of homonyms for members to consult during the week. Then, when members relate one of the homonym meanings to a theme or episode they recall, they are advised to apply the meaning of the *unintended* sound-mate to the same reminiscence, and pursue the free association which occurs. Doing so both disrupts the self-assessment and mood originally arising from the reminiscence, and creates an opportunity for reviewers to approach the memory from a novel, inclusive perspective.

Chapter 10 presents a longitudinal paradox that minimizes reviewers' own entanglement in toxic issues and triangles by emphasizing, instead, the transmission of scripted behavior over generations. This perspective begins by acknowledging the issues currently roiling relationships between the family's two youngest generations, e.g., between reviewers' children and grandchildren.

Then, as members of life review groups move up a generation, they apply this understanding to how these very issues played out between themselves and their children. Since these reminiscences often evoke the conflicting emotions that accompany reviewers' assessment of themselves as parents, facilitators urge reviewers to proceed another generation back, recalling how comparable issues occurred in their relationship with their own parents. Again, to transcend judgments about their parents' behavior, reviewers need to proceed back one generation further, and reflect upon memories and anecdotes about interactions between their father and his parents and their mother and her parents.

The *paradox of attending to the family transmission of scripts* tempers the severity with which reviewers evaluate themselves and others. They see how they behaved in the very fashion that they had criticized in previous generations. The extenuating circumstances surrounding the flow do not excuse irresponsible behavior. They do, though, arouse compassion for themselves and those in other generations.

Chapter 11 presents two paradoxes that move reviewers to attend to their *metaphysical self*. These paradoxes, *Mystical Night* and *Engaged Detachment*, appear in each of the Christian, Hindu, Islamic, Judaic, and Taoist mystical traditions to convey the inclusive, welcoming meaning metaphysical self gives to life. The paradoxes engage reviewers in reflecting upon an explanation of self beyond the purview of the physical and social sciences. Reviewers are typically intrigued both by the theme of mysticism and by learning about traditions with which they are unfamiliar.

Following the text and organized chapter by chapter are lists of references for the sources cited and for recommended readings. The chapters include excerpts from forty-two life reviews that illustrate the developmental concepts and paradoxes under discussion. I have changed names and affiliations, and conflated several reviews into one to protect the anonymity of the reviewers.

No, the past is not at all past.

Chapter One

Reminiscence and Life Review

Now has descended a serener hour,
And with inconstant fortune, friends return;
Though suffering leaves the knowledge and the power
Which says: Let scorn be not repaid with scorn.
—To Mary [1]

Shelley's trenchant lines unfold the themes of this chapter. Older adults have been reminiscing throughout their life, plentifully during their adolescence and then through their succeeding decades. Now, however, during the physiological descent of their later decades, retirement, and the recasting of family roles may occasion "a serener hour." This calm sometimes eases a flood of reminiscing and life review. Even more often the calm is the fruit of these activities.

Reminiscences include the long term memories that older adults may spontaneously slip into when even small experiences at the periphery of attention evoke reverie, reflection, or dreams guiding them into their past. Other times reminiscences are accomplishments as older adults intentionally recover them for reservoirs of entertaining tales and for problem-solving precedents relevant to issues now at hand. These reminiscences are usually vivid, accompanied by pleasant or uncomfortable emotions varying in intensity. The memories may focus upon any period of the life cycle and any aspect of life. The process may be solitary or shared with listeners.

Reminiscing does not evoke an objective, photographic image of past events. There is a plasticity to memories. They are more creative reconstructions of events that accommodate a person's current emotional needs. "Creative reconstruction" is an apt expression connoting that the process is likely to be spontaneous and only partially conscious. It is different from "deceitful," "lying," or "pathologically distorted" accounts.

1

Reminiscences recover the past, with the understanding that the reviewer's mood and needs of the moment affect the accuracy of what is recalled. Consider, for example, the elderly raconteur who in good faith does not let the facts interfere with a good story as she competes at a family reunion with her grandchildren's tales of college life.

Retirement and increasing age-related decrements increase incidents of reminiscing. Retirement, by severing older adults from significant, gratifying roles and relationships, endows memories of seemingly trivial events with value beyond their original character. These memories remain as the principal links to a person's identity before retirement. Some intentionally reminisce about former occupational and social roles to claim role parity or superiority with others upon whom they are now dependent. Similarly, identification with the competence and self-determination that characterized their performance in earlier decades tempers the painful constriction of personal autonomy arising now from failing physical capacities and patronizing societal expectations toward older adults. The increasing proximity of death enables reminiscing to become a form of anticipatory grief work and a part of letting go.

Sister Bridget

I saw the functions of reminiscing play out vividly one day when I was the facilitator for a group of nuns in their eighties who resided, with nursing attention, in their New England motherhouse. During a break for lunch I received a call from Sister Bridget who was attending by video from her room, and who wanted to discuss a question that came up during our sessions. I took this opportunity to visit each of the sisters whose conditions kept them from attending in person. When I visited Sister Bridget, she was sitting in her room, the walls covered with vibrant water colored landscapes. Pointing with hands disfigured by rheumatoid arthritis, she spoke enthusiastically about the locations and periods in her life when she created them:

> *I began painting fifty years ago when I went to Florida to teach the children of migrant workers. For a few hours each evening art restored me to cope with the changes in climate, acquiring the academic resources for our classes, and with outreach to link these families with community services. I was a fledging artist who brought with me a slew of self-help books about this avocation.*
>
> *Seven years later mother superior recalled me to the motherhouse for some R-and-R before I began a new mission. Our handyman met me at the station and loaded my baggage into the van. Don't you know that mother superior asked to meet with me the next day, not about the new assignment but about my luggage! She remarked that the handy man had said of me, "Sr.*

*Bridget set the record for the most stuff he had ever carried." It seemed to the
superior that the weight of my luggage must be incompatible with the simple
living required by our vow of poverty.*

*Now, I'm ordinarily a reticent person, not one to speak up when there's a
fuss, and certainly not to authority figures. I tend to rehearse what I want to
say whenever it is emotionally loaded. But this time, my shock tumbled the
words out spontaneously, "Seven years of paintings! Books, paints, and
unused canvasses! I didn't know that our vows were now a matter of weighing
and measuring." "That will be all, sister," she replied. I left, continued
painting, and the topic was never an issue again.*

*I'm telling you all this because I'm taking heart from this memory. We
have a new nurse here who is rough when she moves and bathes me. I've
hesitated about complaining to her because I depend on her so, but recalling
how I spoke to mother superior is changing things. This nurse is small
potatoes next to her. Yes, the next time the nurse is in here, I'm going to speak
up for myself.*

I checked that night, and she had. Her reminiscing showed, indeed, how
"suffering left the knowledge" that was empowering her now.

LIFE REVIEW

Life Review is a form of reminiscence in which older adults gradually
reconstruct and assess their past, using their current values to judge behavior
that their memories progressively return to consciousness. It focuses
attention upon the connectedness of their past with their current sense of
themselves, and evokes memories of formative experiences that influenced
their personal development. Caught up in the immediate, fluid nature that
characterizes reminiscing, reviewers feel both the emotions that originally
accompanied incidents long past and the emotions that reflect their current
assessment of those events. Members often applaud one another's readiness
to return in reminiscences to troubling events despite the discomfort
involved.

Older adults carry out their life review in their own ways. Some may be
highly aware that they are examining their past, others may feel vaguely
compelled to mull over their past, and still others may almost inadvertently
become engaged in life review. Some keep their reflections a private,
introspective experience, but in doing, so they appraise their past without the
salutary feedback that could modify their interpretation of events. Others
may obsessively retell tales of times past. Most often, life review involves
reviewers and listeners in a give-and-take exchange situated somewhere
between these extremes.

The goal of life review is integrating these recollections in an acceptance of oneself here and now. Achieving such self-acceptance is a task with several dimensions. Looking toward the past, it requires the willingness of older adults to take responsibility for their life story while locating it within the historical and cultural context which conditioned its progression. Looking at the present, it draws upon their ability to savor still the satisfactions that they derived throughout the life cycle, and to forgive themselves for the harm they did and the good they did not do. Looking toward the future, it includes their capacity to anticipate their needs and plan for the most satisfying ways to meet them.[2] These tasks are implicit in Shelley's allusion that the "suffering" which life review discloses "leaves the knowledge and the power" to achieve self-acceptance. This suffering hopefully leaves as well the great-heartedness to "let scorn be not repaid with scorn."

It is not surprising, then, that life review peaks during the fifth decade and continues its high incidence thereafter. Middle age, with its attending sensory decrements, decreases in stamina and sometimes chronic debilitating conditions intimating personal mortality, is a natural catalyst for life review. Again, preparations for retirement ordinarily precipitate life review, since withdrawal from employment so often entails some loss of identity and a threat to self-esteem.

Mr. Skyler

Mr. Skyler's story is a case in point. He shared it during a session of the life review group that met in his local senior center. He had introduced himself to the group by his last name alone and addressed the other participants with the same formality. He was on a first name basis only with family members and very close friends.

Both of his parents had died in their mid-sixties from lung cancer, and he had begun to suffer immobilizing panic attacks when he approached their ages. He also mentioned that he felt the strain of career changes he was making at that time. Mr. Skyler told the group:

> *You probably think of me as some fuddy-duddy for addressing you as "Mr."*
> *and "Ms." and expecting you to do the same with me. Here are my reasons.*
> *The murders of the three civil rights workers in Mississippi during the 1960s*
> *moved me to pursue a social work career, even though I had had few*
> *associations with African-Americans and no first-hand familiarity with*
> *poverty. After completing internships in agencies sponsored by the War on*
> *Poverty as preparation for my graduate degree, I found my first position at a*
> *day care center for children of low income families. In order to make an*
> *appointment to visit the families at home, I stayed after hours to meet each*
> *parent picking up a child.*

When I introduced myself to one mother and addressed her as "Mrs.," she said she preferred that I call her by her nick-name. I thought that doing it her way was "empowering her," so I agreed, and asked her to call me by my first name. When I brought up the idea of a home visit, however, she became anxious. She replied that her husband was extremely jealous, and that I needed to have this conversation with him.

Just then, as I was accompanying her out of my office to find her daughter, he showed up to drive them home. I introduced myself to him, and told him of my conversation with his wife. Without any thought I used her nick-name each time I referred to her. He appeared amiable and we made an appointment for a home visit.

At the day care center the next morning, the director told me that the husband had been arrested. A neighbor had seen him run his wife down with his car. He was convicted of the crime. No hard evidence for a motive was found. But I've never doubted that my using his wife's nick-name after being alone with her in my office had fired his imagination. I believe that my thoughtlessness triggered her death.

I did not want this tragedy to be purposeless. I sought to counsel the daughter, but her grandparents had taken her out of state to live with them. I entered psychotherapy, and sought out the most challenging supervisors and consultants to mentor me. But I still get terribly anxious with people unless I keep relationships on a formal, last name basis.

By my fifties I was an experienced worker in a sequence of visionary, experimental programs to help single-parent families find opportunities to achieve some minimal standards of living with decency. During this time my panic attacks began, perhaps because of my parents' history and also because I saw that I was not going to accomplish my goals if I remained a social worker.

To make system-level changes, I decided I needed to become a lawyer. So I resigned, went into debt, studied in the basement, and began a career with the Equal Opportunity Commission. But at what cost! I traveled incessantly. My wife divorced me because I paid so little attention to our relationship and had virtually abandoned our children.

I think everything that's happened has been a wake-up call for me, and this group is helping me answer the phone. I'm really nervous, but I want to try out our first names now. I see how I've used formality to avoid coping with that murder years ago. And let me thank you for the give-and-take I've heard here which has given me a plan. All those years I was busy trying to climb higher ladders faster and faster. Now I see that I had them against the wrong walls. Letter by letter and phone call by phone call, I am going to try to rebuild my family ties. And as for us, please call me Bob.

The group's history of attentive support eases Bob to expand his reminiscence from the initial trauma to consequent errors in judgment to current dissatisfactions. His own attentiveness to others has evoked a self-awareness that he is eager to share. Reentering his past and discussing it moves him to bear the anxiety that accompanies the risks of acting informally and of reconnecting with his family.

GROUP FACILITATORS

Facilitators are responsible for designing their life review groups. They determine the number of participants (no more than seven), the length of sessions (no more than ninety minutes), and the number of sessions (open ended). They may choose groups that meet independently, or that meet as extensions of adult education courses, retreats, or field trips.

Facilitators are responsible for advertizing their groups. The announcements should emphasize the social and instructional character of the groups. These are not group therapy sessions. When facilitators present the groups as available on a "first come" basis, the participants' backgrounds are more likely to be heterogeneous and mutually enriching.

Facilitators must be able to share their knowledge about the role of reminiscing in the life of older adults, and give examples from their own life (regardless of their age). They should be able to determine the appropriateness of using paradoxes when reviewers are "memory stuck," and explain with examples how paradoxes advance reminiscing.

Facilitators, of course, must be skilled in promoting group dynamics. They want the participants themselves to draw out the memories of the shy, to limit the loquacious, to support one another. They want to ensure that everyone feels so safe and valued that they can attend open heartedly and respond empathically to each other.

Facilitators are key in ensuring that life review becomes a renewal, an initiation opening new vistas.

Chapter Two

Self as Maturation

Year after year beheld the silent toil
That spread his lustrous coil;
Still as the spiral grew,
He left the past year's dwelling for the new,
Stole with soft step its shining archways through,
Built up its idle door,
Stretched in his last-found home, and knew the old no more.
—*The Chambered Nautilus* [1]

No matter how the social sciences examine it, the self remains a paradox. It is the basis for individuality, that taken-for-granted "sense of being an independent center of initiative and perception."[2] At the same time, it is truly a composite of the ideals, attitudes, and competencies internalized from others. Self is the inner source of freedom and creativity, yet families assign each self by distributing ancient scripts for roles that they need members to play. Moreover, the social sciences examine self from many view points, yet they cannot comprehend self's metaphysical core.

Then, in life review the self assesses itself remembered. This is a dynamic process because the self-assessing-self creatively reconstructs the self remembered. The process is further complicated because every person possesses several selves simultaneously. The next three chapters find meaning in this paradox by assessing the expansion and constraints on self-esteem arising from the several perspectives on the development of self.

THE EPIGENETIC SELF

The *epigenetic self* refers to the life long process of integrating a sequence of *maturational selves*.[3] Maturation is the personal advance that results from concurrent physiological, neurological, and psychological development. Ideally, at each level of maturation persons can draw upon resources in the environment to demonstrate the new abilities now available to them. They can use their emerging knowledge and skills to manage the challenges at their current stage of development, and prime themselves for coping with the challenges at the next stage. In effect, persons subsume the competencies from all the preceding levels to support them in succeeding at the newest level of maturation.

Oliver Wendell Holmes portrays this model in his account of the *Chambered Nautilus*. He captures the lengthy time frame that maturation requires and the teleology that no single chamber is an end in itself. The model exceeds the poem in one respect, however. The model preserves access to the resources of earlier levels, while the poem seals each chamber as the next is built.

OBSERVANT-SELF

Children begin to internalize the earliest maturational self, the *observant-self*, even prior to language. This primitive construct is not initially present at birth, but emerges as they identify with the attitudes of parents, kin, and significant others. In doing this, the observant-self maintains a continuity of learned beliefs, goals, ideals, and skills.

When caretakers' expectations are appropriate and conveyed empathically, they further children's sense of wellbeing, and form a foundation for subsequent maturational selves. There are, however, many situations that can interfere with the expression or reception of empathy: when children's temperaments strongly predispose them to fright reactions; when caretakers' responses are not consistent, e.g., ambivalence toward the fourth female child born before the long awaited birth of a boy (or vice-versa); when the environment does not provide enough security, e.g., being born at the site of warfare or in the throes of an economic depression. A confluence of these factors can threaten a secure sense of self, and at times even arrest psychological development at the level of the observant-self.

WANT-TO-BE-SELF

Maturation then moves adolescents to the *want-to-be-self* they wish to become.[4] Ideally, this self includes early stirrings of inclusiveness found in "the ability to feel connected with others, implicated in their lives."[5] This self also alerts adolescents to recognize peer group and institutional expectations supportive of their best interests, to repudiate expectations found irreconcilable, and temper others in service to their ideals. There is the risk, however, that the observant-self may obscure the want-to-be-self by subverting ideals into oppressive and unrealizable standards.

COMPETENT-SELF

After age twenty-five or so, maturation moves young adults to integrate these earlier selves within a *competent-self.* This maturational self manages both the interpersonal activities and the intrapersonal processes through which young adults express their continuity of self over the life cycle.[6] The competent-self affirms young adults as having "a place in the world, the right to express themselves, and the power to affect and participate in what happens" to them.[7] When the competent-self subsumes the other maturational selves in an integrated sequence, young adults can manage the transition from school to employment, from one career to another, from natal home to a residence of their own, and from single life to an informed, respectful decision to enter into marriage or a committed relationship.

If young adults do not successfully integrate their maturational selves, however, they are likely to settle for "getting by," recycling internalized standards without reflecting upon their appropriateness, or unwittingly living out parental dreams instead of their own. Moreover, if they try to distance themselves from their family of origin in order to minimize the anxiety arising from their involvement in family issues, they invariably bring that unresolved sensitivity into other emotionally charged relationships.

INCLUSIVE-SELF

Maturation next moves mature adults toward an *inclusive-self* with an ever widening awareness of people's lifelong interdependence upon one another. This self can appreciate how personal characteristics are rooted more in relationships than exclusively within an individual. Walt Whitman succinctly expressed this point in his *Song of Myself,* "Every atom belonging to me as good belongs to you."[8]

Inclusive-self moves adults to altruistic efforts that assuage suffering, further social justice, and benefit future generations. Those who have inadequately managed their sequence of selves, however, can subvert their inclusive-self either by slighting their own unmet needs or by compulsively "doing good" in order to "feel good."

All these selves persist through life on a continuum of success both in meeting the challenges each stage presents and in forming a facilely integrated sequence. When this integration does not occur, maturational selves inadequately developed impede, and sometimes sabotage, the management of life tasks at the current stage.

An excerpt of Laura's life review follows as an example of a balky, tortuous process of maturation.

Laura

Laura, a vigorous sixty-nine year old widow with one daughter, was recently dismissed after ten years as a grammar school crossing guard.

> *It was so unfair. My supervisor called me in and played me the videotape she had secretly made of me at work. She complained that I was still holding up traffic after the kids were all on the sidewalk. She went on that the bigger the vehicles were, the longer I kept them stopped. O.K., maybe I was showing them that they couldn't intimidate me, but never, not once, in my ten years was a child ever hurt. The kids love me. The ones from way back even hug me when they come home from college. They'll never hire another guard as sharp as me standing in the middle of the street holding my STOP sign up.*
>
> *Authorities always hold it against me when I make my own practical decisions. Most of my life I worked as a matron in a university's faculty office building. I was "Laura" to everyone, but they were all "Doctor-this" or "Professor-that," and left their offices a mess for me to clean up. So I decided to make things more equal. Whenever new faculty arrived, I introduced myself as "Ms. Laura" and addressed them as "Dr. Barbara" or "Dr. Ron." There wasn't any trouble until some of the old timers asked my supervisor what was going on. She got on my case, and threatened to fire me unless this stopped. I have to eat; so I stopped.*
>
> *It is so hard when you have no one to back you up. For instance, what I went through to get married! Since my father worked enormous hours, I really was with him only on the weekends. Any time the weather was decent, he'd take my mother and me out in his sail boat. Half the time I got seasick, and all the time I was bored. When I protested that I wanted to be with my friends, he said to bring them along. Here I was a grown woman, and I had to keep my social life to myself for privacy. When I finally did bring my (secret) fiancé aboard the boat, my father trapped him and gave him the third degree.*

The day came when my mother's mom couldn't cook dinner, bathe, and get settled for the night by herself anymore, so I offered to move in with her. When she died, I took over her apartment and got a job that paid the rent. My fiancé and I eloped, kept our marriage quiet, and lived together in the apartment. When my pregnancy started to show, though, we had to tell my folks. My mother was broken hearted that our wedding was not a big event, and my father was so incensed that we had acted without his approval that he did not talk to us until the baby arrived.

My father was never a walk in the park. Mother was much easier to talk when I wanted something. I remember the time she lifted some coins from his collection. She was determined to get enough change to buy me a new blouse for starting high school. She was also the one I had gone to after tenth grade, begging to be allowed to drop out of school. She said there was no chance my father would ever agree. So I stayed. I didn't learn much, but I graduated.

You see, I had learned way back that there was no arguing with my father. My name is Laura because my father expected my first name to be Laurence and my middle name Bradley. Through my childhood my parents chided me when I misbehaved by saying, "Laurence Bradley would not have acted like that!" That made me wonder why I didn't have a middle name too. So I tried out lots of them, but each time my father told me, "Your name is Laura, and that's that."

Laura's account proceeds from the present through earlier stages of maturation. She does not approximate the goal for any stage, and her inability to integrate the stages leaves her with little insight about proceeding more constructively. The following account, on the other hand, provides a more articulated, sanguine example of integrating maturational selves.

Zirdra

Zirdra, a seventy-one year old taxi driver, drew an example of a successful epigenetic model from her own life review:

I've been driving for eight years now, ever since I retired from working as a pharmacist. It gets me off my feet and gives me the chance to chat with lots of different people. Since I live in a neighborhood that's moved from having one nationality to many, I've been using tapes to learn Spanish, and I practice it with many of my passengers.

In two respects I know what it means to be from another culture, and what a difference others' support can make. Our parents had escaped from Soviet occupied Latvia in 1948, settled in the United States, and raised us in a church where all the services were in Latvian. During college in another state I became certain that I was a lesbian. I hesitated telling my parents because there seemed to be no other homosexuals that they knew. Only after I graduated with my pharmacy degree, and met the woman I've lived with for my adult life, did I tell my parents. My mother said, "We've thought as much. Please be true to yourself." My father added, with a suppressed smile, "I only hope your partner is Latvian."

In fact, my family has rooted for me all my life. When I was fifteen, I confided in my seventeen year old sister about a topic I was going to raise during dinner. My sister had become fluent in Latvian, and sang in the choir. But I was embarrassed when my non-Latvian classmates would overhear my parents speaking the language, and I did not want to sing in the choir. I asked her to support me when I spoke up. "No big deal," she said. "Different strokes for different folks."

When I finally brought up language and religion that evening, I picked up on my sister's point. I told my parents that I didn't have my sister's gift for singing, and I'd like to go to services in English. They said they thought I could sing well enough, but the choir should be a labor of love, not of duty. If I didn't want to join, so be it. They added that they could see that their generation or mine might be the last to continue the services in Latvian, that assimilation could not be denied. They proposed that until I was eighteen I should accompany them three Sundays a month. I could go with my friends to their churches on the remaining Sunday. I agreed, and eventually made my own choice to stay in the Latvian church. Now I'm a member on the transition committee for merging our church with another, larger congregation.

Even when I was in kindergarten, my parents guided me instead of forcing me. My father came once dressed up as Santa Claus, but I recognized his shoes. I told my mother how he fooled my classmates, and how I was going to tell them the next day that it was only my father. She explained to me that I could ruin their Christmas if I did not keep the secret, but I could tell my father at dinner that I had spotted him. So, that night when he asked about my day, I started my answer with, "Ho, Ho, Ho!!"

Reminiscing, then, challenges older adults to accept their entire epigenetic self in an inclusive, compassionate review, leaving "the past year's dwelling for the new." Zirdra is one of many older adults who can recall the exhilarating, humorous, poignant, or tragic incidents that were "in synch" or "at odds" with their maturational selves at each stage. "Each self," she once noted, "is a way I *do* me, but not the *only* way I do me." Her maturation is, indeed, in synch.

Chapter Three

Self as Script

The world stands out on either side
No wider than the heart is wide;
Above the world is stretched the sky,—
No higher than the soul is high.
The heart can push the sea and land
Farther away on either hand;
The soul can split the sky in two,
And let the face of God shine through.
But East and West will pinch the heart
That cannot keep them pushed apart.
And he whose soul is flat—the sky
Will cave in on him bye and bye.—Renascence [1]

The first two, often three, stages of the epigenetic self ordinarily emerge within the give-and-take, the structure, and demeanor of family living. This intergenerational context passes on the family scripts that largely prescribe the life long characteristics of each member's self. Edna St. Vincent Millay identifies these scripted characteristics with the dimensions of heart and soul hopefully ready to respond to life.

FAMILY SCRIPTS[2]

"Self" is an aggregate term embracing the interplay of family dynamics over many generations. A latent purpose inherent in family relationships is perpetuating the family identity by replicating traits in members of subsequent generations. Siblings, cousins, and other kin within the extended family then live out roles which, for better and worse, have been significant in the lives of their predecessors.

The transmission of family identity occurs when older generations assign younger members "scripts" for parts in the long running family drama. The integrity of the drama then weighs upon members to remain in character as they play out the family's recurrent issues. Members can elaborate upon their parts, enter and withdraw from the stage on their own initiative, and improvise their lines. To varying degrees, families provide latitude in these respects, so long as members remain true to their character and provide one another with the cues they need to play upon the family stage. Family identity, individual scripts, and ongoing issues, then, are inseparably entwined.

INTERGENERATIONAL TRANSMISSION

Whenever new members, such as spouses and children, enter a family, eleven criteria appear especially prominent during the "auditions" that match these members with family based scripts:

Biological Inheritance[3]

Children's awareness of their physical appearance; handicap; singular gender, complexion, eye or hair color, height, weight and handedness; relative intellectual, cultural, and physical prowess; resemblance to specific relatives- all affect the scripts assigned and accepted. Hannah, for instance, reminisced that she was the oldest child and only daughter with three brothers.

> *My mother would repeat that my birth occurred the day after my matriarchal grandmother, "the Contessa," died. She also told me I had striking green eyes which others noticed because my left eye socket was set just slightly higher than my right. Once I was ten, I was left in charge of my brothers until supper time. Whenever they gave me a hard time, I threatened them with the power of my "evil eye." I had many suitors; all of them complimented my eyes. I was not only in charge; I was a future Contessa in rehearsal.*

To use Millay's metaphor, Hannah would become adept at "pinching" many of her kin.

Sibling Constellations

Similarities in gender and ordinal positions between parents and children often affect the kinds of behavior presented to each child. Parents are more likely to identify with that child of the same sex who has an ordinal position similar to their own. They are also more likely to project upon their other children the feelings they hold toward their own siblings of the same gender and position as the children's. Thus, the quality of relationships among siblings in one generation patterns the quality of relationships among siblings in the following generation. Dieter offered an example from his reminiscence.

> *I was born between two sisters. My younger sister was quiet, and usually buried in some book. My older sister was something else! She was forever in "Notice Me" mode, continually strutting about her part in some grammar school play, a science prize in high school, or a Congressional internship in college. Meanwhile, I was only getting by in school, and on the junior varsity soccer team.*
>
> *So didn't I have four children, girl, boy, girl, boy, and really came into my own when my first son arrived. I gave him his first soccer ball. I went to all his games. But I didn't do right by his older sister. Of course, I spent time with her doing homework, and we bought ice cream sundaes to celebrate her report cards. She let me know, though, that she had felt slighted all along. Early one date night she commented, "When you're talking to the fellow, Dad, you'll remember my name, right?"*

Dieter's account shows him living out the script for a smarting, competitive middle child.

Boundaries between Generations and among Family Members

Too permeable boundaries enmesh children in triangles by encouraging them to take one side between estranged parents, siblings, or between sets of grandparents. These boundaries, moreover, condition children to grow up as "emotional pursuers," invading others' boundaries, pushing advice, demanding attention, and engulfing the space required for rational problem-solving.

So too do impermeable boundaries facilitate triangles by cutting children off from adequate communication, feedback, and support. These boundaries condition children to grow up as "emotional distancers," erecting rigid boundaries around themselves by withdrawing to impersonal activities and using humor, denial, or silence as diversions from effective conflict resolution.

Children of either group tend also to develop further rigidities. Some may become "over-functioners," impatiently carrying out others' responsibilities, regarding themselves as expeditious, but, in fact, denying the opportunity for others to test their own problem-solving skills. Others, dubious about their ability to function productively and anticipating being overwhelmed with anxiety, may become "under-functioners," handling responsibilities, completing tasks, and sustaining relationships in a desultory or halting manner.

Role Modeling

Cyrus retired prematurely from his years as a medical missionary due to nervous exhaustion. When he reminisced about his reasons for having chosen his career he invariably mentioned his father's example.

> *When my father walked with me to and from my kindergarten classes, he repeatedly stooped to pick up rusting nails and shards of glass from the sidewalk, "So they can't hurt anyone." His continual emphasis on being accommodating, helpful, and maintaining pleasant relationships made the point that a prompt response to people's needs was never enough by itself. I needed to anticipate people's needs and remove the obstacles to their progress. Eventually it all became too much.*

As Cyrus lived out the script for an anxious, over-responsible self, his collapse was so complete that, in Millay's terms, even "the sky caved in on him bye and bye."

Emotionally Loaded Terms

Monique remembered that when she was growing up her relatives used derogatory terms to refer to Jews.

> *I even heard my mother, who spoke ill of no one, call Jews "Eskimos." She stopped the practice when I asked her for an explanation, but this puzzling designation conveyed to me that Jews must somehow be "very different." As an adult and a civil rights activist for racially integrated education, I worked regularly in inter-group functions with many Jews experienced in this field. I think my activism, too often brittle and driven, was in part a reaction to my family's prejudices. "Heads or tails—I'm still paying with the same family coin."*

Indeed, Monique has been living out the family script for her rebellious, idealistic self.

Family Folklore

Family folklore is a repository of ancestors' behavior that transmits to subsequent generations unquestioned models of expected performance. It often memorializes in a chain of anecdotes the participation of kin in national and international events, such as, emigration, military service, economic depression, natural catastrophes, union organizing, or social protests. The criterion for judging their behavior is usually the fidelity with which kin maintained family values and rules as they participated in these larger scenes.

Kin also use folklore to denigrate as disloyalty or eccentricity a member's efforts at self-actualization that disturb the balance among family relationships. They may point to an ancestor's disgrace or comeuppance for pursuing a course similar to the one a member is considering now. Thus, tampering with a script can provoke vague, age old taboos that circumscribe the limits of acceptable behavior.

Names and Nicknames

Connotations associated with children's names and nicknames can ease them into specific scripts. Kin, for instance, may look for children who are named after others in the family to repeat or exceed the accomplishments of their namesakes. Often enough "when families fight about whose forebears or whose side of the family the child will be named after, they're also arguing about the role they need or want this child to play."[4] Jo's reminiscences include a telling example:

> *My mother named me Irena after a famous violinist. She followed up by starting my violin lessons when I was four. I continued them and had an orchestral career until I began raising my own family of seven children. But I had an athletic gene from my dad's side, and I began playing handball early on. Because I am ambidextrous, I could even beat boys older than myself. My mother didn't want me "acting like a tomboy," but her mother said I'd outgrow it.*
>
> *Grandma had seen the movie "Gigi" in which the vigorous female lead grows up to be a polished young woman. When she started calling me Gigi, every one followed suit. But when I was in high school, my parents agreed that that was no name for a concert violinist. So my younger brothers quipped that I should be G.I. (Gigi Irena). That led to G.I. Joe and finally to Jo. I think of Jo as my "freedom name," liberating me to play both on the violin and on the slopes where I ski.*

To use Millay's imagery, her nickname "split the sky in two, and let the face of God shine through," enabling her to live out the script for her expansive, "I want it all" self.

Family Slogans

Locking her car doors before pulling out of the driveway, Deborah observed, "Better to be safe than sorry." Wearing a visor to screen the sun, Caleb began to scrape paint chips off the floor of the porch. "You know how it is, 'Idle hands are the devil's workshop.'" Stylishly attired as always, Yolanda declined a second éclair with a muffled aside, "A second on the lips; forever on the hips."

These aphorisms alert children to their family's script for the "good life." Such expressions convey parental attitudes about an unlimited array of topics: enjoying one's body; the importance of appearances, or of being educated, wealthy, or religious; expressing caring and anger; using leisure time and savings; and acceptable forms of self-expression.

Epitaphs

"She married outside the faith." "He wouldn't spend a nickel to see an earthquake." "He never visited his parents." "She had a drinking problem for years." In each case a family member uses a brief statement, without qualifiers or elaboration, to summarize another person's life. It is irrelevant whether the person summarily labeled is alive or dead. The epitaph conveys the judgment that the speaker has made about another. The tenacity of epitaphs and the limited criteria used for assessing the worth of another person make the impact of epitaphs intimidating.

Family Secrets

Many adults report the confusion they experienced as children or young adults upon learning about a family secret. They were annoyed, of course, that kin had not trusted them enough to act responsibly with this information. When the secret concerned events that impacted heavily upon their own formation, they were especially outraged that the secrecy had prevented them from influencing this impact. Secrets may support a shared fiction that the family is unusually harmonious and loving while preventing members from gathering a more realistic understanding of their family. The reminiscence that Cedric shared revealed how a secret managed a touchy relationship.

> *I'm the younger of two sons, and I look like my mother's dad Brian. I'm more quiet and laid back like him, and not a showman like my father's dad Cedric. Yet I'm named after Cedric and even have him as my godfather. My brother is also named after a relative on my father's side. I've suspected that there was no love lost between my mother and her in-laws, so I was puzzled how the given names from my father's side prevailed.*

> *But I found out the answer when my brother and I visited England after our parents died. My mother's father had emigrated from "the back of beyond" in rural England, and with great effort we came upon the family homestead. In the cemetery nearby a headstone listed my maternal great-grandfather's name: Cedric. My mother and her parents kept this relationship to themselves so that my father's side would be flattered enough to keep the peace. The deception by silence satisfied my mother.*

Not surprisingly Cedric's life story went on to show how he lived out the script for his mediating, "don't ruffle feathers" self.

Lectures

Lectures convey family honed values to which the speakers are deeply committed. Often an incident dramatizing these values precipitates a corresponding lecture. The emotional intensity with which it is given, the awkward pauses and nonverbal signals of discomfort that accompany emotionally loaded topics like sexuality, or the formal stiffness of the presentation, all convey the earnestness that is compressed into the lecture. Rosalynn's reminiscence is a case in point:

> *During the morning of my fourteenth birthday my mother sat next to me on the sofa, cleared her throat, and said she wanted to bring up something I should keep in mind when I became fond of a young man. She advised me to notice whether he or members of his family had webbing between their fingers or toes or under their armpits. I should end the relationship if they did, 'cause she knew a friend who had a baby by a man with such appendages, and the infant was disfigured and died. When my mother finished, she didn't ask if I had questions. She got up, and finished the arrangements for my party. And I didn't ask any questions 'cause I thought that what she said was the closest my mom could come to giving me any sex instruction!*

Rosalynn's mother was tutoring her how to live out the script for a bowdlerized self, attentive to the nonverbal, contextual cues in others' statements.

Older adults have never left their families because they contain their families within their "heart" and "soul." Life review is an opportunity for them to recognize the parameters that their families set, nudge these limits more expansively, and ideally respond with wonder and some degree of good humor. In these cases, their review is an able foundation for planning their future.

Chapter Four

Self as Metaphysical

*If people become bad, that is not the fault of their
nature. All people naturally feel compassion and shame;
all people naturally regard others with respect; all people
naturally love goodness and hate evil. . . . These qualities are
not welded on to a person; they are present in everyone.—The Book of Mencius* [1]

The preceding chapters have presented a socially constructed self. This chapter elaborates upon a spiritual, metaphysical self. As Meng Tzu's reflection indicates, metaphysical self is the natural, universal foundation for qualities inherent in human beings. Though introspection cannot comprehend the metaphysical self in its essence, this self remains for all a sanctuary, a source of unconditional acceptance, an assurance "of being loved and lovable, valued and valuable as we are, regardless of what we do."[2]

From a humanistic point of view the metaphysical self refers to people's relationship to their life force as "an Earthling growing naturally out of the Universe."[3] It is the ultimate source continually nourishing consciousness, ideals, personality, accomplishment, and interconnectedness. It is an unfathomable, swelling wellspring sustaining existence-as-gift and is the basis for self-esteem, focusing on *being* rather than *doing.*

One older adult summarized her understanding of metaphysical self with this analogy:

> *I see this self as the "ground," with its nutrient-bearing streams, that enlivens the seeds of our personal development. Rooted in this ground, all of us develop our potential, become fruitful trees. Uprooted, unable to draw upon the resources of self, we are so many boards, sticks. But to appreciate this rootedness, we need the perspective that we are part of an orchard. Others' shade, spacing, and purpose are integral to our fruition.*

21

Dominique

Dominique responded to the imagery of the ground and the orchard with her own account of metaphysical self. She is an eighty-four year old divorcee, retired after a career as a secondary school English teacher. Her advanced placement class was consistently oversubscribed in good part because of her reputation for biting asides about members of her ex-husband's family, amplified with acerbic judgments, wry humor, and liberal doses of sarcasm.

> *When I retired, of course I lost my student audience. I also began going to the funerals of many people who had been the butt of my stories. I saw these events as opportunities to gloat, even if people resented my being there. But at each funeral there would be some mourner who was genuinely pleased to see me, and who brought up anecdotes that showed how much they admired some kindness or steadfastness of the deceased.*
>
> *After a while, I saw that both their gracious stories and the warmth shown me arose from the empathy of these mourners. I had stored what I knew of the deceased as grist for humor and put-downs. I paid attention to people so that I'd "have the goods on them." Empathy wasn't part of my repertoire.*
>
> *Now I'm attentive in our own group because I want to sense how it is to be someone else. I've even been answering your questions about my life review. And you have my word that what I learn in our group goes no further than me. Even in the memories I've shared with you, I think I've saved most of the barbs for my own behavior. You see, something's been going on inside me.*

What is going on is no secret. Dominique is getting in touch with the metaphysical self that others are showing her nourishes them all.

METAPHYSICAL SELF ACROSS TRADITIONS[4]

From a religious point of view, the metaphysical self refers to the self immersed in the Absolute at "the depths of people's hearts where neither sin nor desire nor self-knowledge can reach, the core of their reality, the person that each one is in God's eyes."[5] As a consequence, peoples' self-esteem proceeds from God's esteem for them, and their self-knowledge from an awareness of their self as known by God. From this perspective, reviewers accept themselves because they have already been accepted. Different religions express this point each in its own idiom.

Islam

Islam, for example, imagines a dialog between the metaphysical self and the socially constructed self which the former enlivens and accepts:

> *One went to the door of the Beloved and knocked. A voice asked, "Who is there?" He answered, "It is I." The voice said, "There is no room for Me and Thee." The door was shut. After a year of solitude and deprivation he returned and knocked. A voice from within asked, "Who is there?" The man said, "It is Thee." The door was opened for him.*[6]

Another aspiration expresses the same acknowledgment of metaphysical self:

> *O God, I possess that mirror in which you are reflected. Rather, I am that mirror. You are not separate from me.*[7]

In a word:

> *God says "that He [sic] is in the heaven and on the earth, that He is with us wherever we are; He is, in essence, us."*[8]

Judaism

Similarly, Jewish mystics convey the same message about the immersion of identity in the metaphysical self:

> *Man's essence is only the soul that is within him, which is a portion of God above. Thus, there is nothing in the entire world except the Holy One.*[9]

Hinduism

Hinduism, in turn, uses the medium of light to emphasize the centrality of the metaphysical self:

> *Every cell of this, my physical body, is filled with Divine Light; every level of consciousness is illumined with Divine Light. The Divine Light penetrates every single cell of my being, every level of consciousness.*[10]

Christianity

Christian mystics reiterate this theme of transcendent intimacy as the core of metaphysical self:

> *The soul is so completely one with God that the one cannot be understood without the other. One can think heat easily enough without fire and the shining without the sun, but God cannot be understood without the soul, nor the soul without God, so utterly are they one.*[11]

Again:

> *Between God and our soul there is neither wrath nor forgiveness. For our soul is so wholly united to God that nothing can interpose.*[12]

In a word:

> *It is God's pleasure and rapture to discover identity, because He [sic] can always put His whole nature into it. For, He is this identity itself.*[13]

The variety of traditions, each with its own idiomatic and metaphorical expression, converges in this common theme that humankind resides in a benevolent deity seeking the self-fulfillment of each person.

Lurleen

Lurleen's story, even without mentioning a higher power, illustrates how she sees this theme play out in her own life. She is eighty-nine years old, the oldest child followed by seven brothers. Her father died when she was fifteen, and she left school to help her mother support the family. When her brothers began supporting her at age seventy-five, she retired from a life time of cleaning houses. She spoke about metaphysical self in these terms:

> *By the time I turned thirty I began spending a little time each night just sitting quietly, and paying attention to whatever sounds I heard. No matter how tired I was, I kept this up all my life. Many a night I fell asleep while I was listening.*
>
> *I noticed even as a teenager that when I wasn't sure what I should do, something like a whisper would advise me. Well, it wasn't a whisper you could hear; more like a nudge or a tiny tightness in my chest. It was easy to ignore, but it was gently guiding me to choose what was best for me.*
>
> *One time, when I was about twenty-five, I had just finished my house cleaning job. It was raining awfully hard, and a friend of the lady's son offered to drive me home. Right away my body said, "Don't go with him," but the storm was louder than this whisper. So, I got in his car, and as we pulled away I noticed there were no door knobs on my side. And the fellow was not heading toward my home. When I told him we were going the wrong way, he said he knew a nice place where we could relax first.*
>
> *I almost died when I heard him, but then I remembered a conversation I had with a neighbor who had epilepsy. She had told me that she could tell when a seizure was coming. So I told the fellow that I had epilepsy, that I felt a convulsion coming, and that I might vomit all over the front seat. It worked! He stopped the car, pushed some button on his side that opened my door, shoved me out and drove off.*
>
> *I couldn't tell my family 'cause my brothers would have hurt him bad. But I made up my mind that I was going to pay more attention to my body, to listen to the whisper however faint it was. My little time each evening helps me "to keep the channels open."*

Lurleen interprets her whisper as emanating from her metaphysical self. Those of us who heard her story think that her readiness both to remain in passive attentiveness at night and especially to protect the driver from her brothers emerge from her metaphysical self as well.

Similarly, life review is an opportunity for older adults to find the metaphysical self real, accessible and potent. This is not automatically the case, however, because accepting the reality of metaphysical self requires passive attentiveness and setting time apart for quiet reflection. Since these characteristics also enrich the process of life review, the fortunate reviewer may achieve both.

Chapter Five

Self-Esteem

Make me thy lyre, ev'n as the forest is:
What if my leaves are falling as its own?
The tumult of thy mighty harmonies
Will take from both a deep autumnal tone.—Ode to the West Wind [1]

Shelley gives poetic expression here to the way older adults with vigorous self-esteem see themselves. In their eyes they are capable, significant, and intrinsically good enough to allow the life reviewed to replenish the life at hand. Asking, "What if my leaves are falling," they look for no exemptions from the vicissitudes of aging, but look to find in them "a deep autumnal tone" of meaning. They scan and assess their personal history from the perspective of an inner-directed, interdependent self, and accept the maturational selves their memories reveal to them. Through the acute lens of this hearty self-esteem they observe and assess themselves with realism, compassion, and self-acceptance.

Those with frail self-esteem, however, evaluate their past from the perspective of an other-directed, indeterminate self that has not adequately integrated earlier stages of development. Older adults with lower levels of self-esteem tend to observe and judge the past with errant harshness.

Self-esteem is the abiding judgment people have made about their competence and worth, the lens through which they review their personal history and discern meaning in their lives.[2] They are likely to take this appraisal of their self-confidence and self-respect for granted because it is a component of all their other feelings as well.

ORIGINS OF SELF-ESTEEM

Self-esteem arises during the early stage of maturation as children navigate their budding selfhood. They internalize the criteria they observe care givers use toward them or believe they have toward them, and evaluate themselves accordingly. School age children and adolescents later endure with peers episodes of self-consciousness, embarrassment, or ridicule. When their family and environment can moderate the intensity of these episodes, adolescents can use them to build appropriate personal boundaries. Their own feelings of being exposed to others' criticism can sensitize adolescents to cues of discomfort in others, and guide them to skirt areas of others' sensitivity. Their tutor is the law of gradualness. They must wait upon maturational opportunities to learn the grammar, develop the muscles, experiment with social skills, and give voice to emerging values—all of which will incrementally and synergistically enable them to carry out adult roles.

Finally, the instructive shame accompanying an inclination to defect from cherished values is an early warning to adolescents that their behavior is likely to diminish their self-esteem. The feeling is a trajectory correction whenever their behavior is going off course. For, so long as they stand inadequate in contrast to their better self, they still can claim that better self.[3]

Once adolescents proceed into young adulthood, these episodes challenge them to accept themselves as "good enough" without needing to manipulate others for continuing confirmation of this self-assessment. They can acknowledge that they are each distinct individuals while remaining members of the community whose ideals they share.

ENHANCING SELF-ESTEEM

Self-esteem exists along a continuum from an optimal level at one end, through decreasing but still instructive and benign levels, through minimal and at times dysfunctional levels, to embedded shame at the other end. Each person's location on the continuum remains basically unaltered through life, unless there is some clinical intervention. There are, however, fluctuations within this stability. There is the accelerated rush of satisfaction people feel when they excel at something, demonstrate elusive talent, or apply expert knowledge. After achieving this peak experience, however, they return to their basic level of self-esteem.

This book does not focus on enabling members of life review groups to accomplish peak experiences. Its purpose, rather, is guiding reviewers in stretching their own capacity to incorporate the frequency, duration, and optimal functioning of five characteristics inherent in robust self-esteem. Even though group members may be unable to sustain this keen level of functioning indefinitely, they will learn the strength of group support, test a variety of paradoxes that revise their thinking, and find self-acceptance in memories that had initially appeared as punitive. The characteristics are:

- Efficacy—competence in coping with tasks and the issues associated with them. Those brimming with efficacy conflate "Yes, you can" and "Know your limits."
- Inner authority—relying upon our own informed conscience, and taking responsibility for our own decisions and actions. It offers the guidance, "Prefer confidence to certainty," thus encouraging both accomplishment and ongoing openness to corrective information.
- Maintenance of firm yet permeable boundaries—including intrapersonal, interpersonal, and transpersonal boundaries. The mantra for those who can calibrate the permeability of boundaries within themselves and among others is "Let there be spaces in your togetherness."[4]
- Openness to risk taking—allowing others and ourselves to make mistakes as a way of learning, and expressing our feelings more frequently and directly.[5] Those with openness conflate, "Oops! What can I learn from this?" and "We need to talk."
- Uniqueness—affirming that "what we do and who we are matters," and thus decreasing any need to compare ourselves with others.[6] Those with a healthy sense of uniqueness conflate, "I do count" and "Don't believe everything you think."

Genevieve

Genevieve is an eighty-seven year old widow whose life review demonstrates these characteristics of hearty self-esteem. When she was nine years old, her family emigrated from Alsace-Lorraine, and settled in rural New York where her father worked on an aqueducts furnishing water for New York City. She married a stone mason who earned a steady but modest income, and who died two decades later the same year as her own mother. At that time she had a fourteen year old son Andre who now lives in Arizona.

Her father was quiet and stern with Genevieve, and expected her to speak to him only with his permission. After she had her own family and he grew enfeebled from injuries, she described their relationship as "courteous and mutually helpful from a distance." She continued her reminiscing:

> *So I had to take more initiative when we both were widowed. I suggested to him that he live with Andre and me. That way I could look out for him, and he could help us out financially. Of course, he wanted to decide on the amount he contributed. Well, when he told me, "I don't want anybody bossing me*

around," I learned that money was not the issue. I was blunt, "I have never told you what to do, and I don't intend to start now." Still, on the day he moved in he carried a life size cardboard cutout of a woman advertizing some brand of soda. He intended to leave it on the porch, as "the only one who doesn't sass me back." "We all need a good friend," I agreed, as I carried it to his room. (Inner Authority)

Those with inner authority neither look to others to create their happiness nor blame others for their own sorrows.[7] The authority emerges from an unconditional self-acceptance that they are innately good enough. Notice how Genevieve acts from a conviction that she should be able to manage her unfortunate situation. She reaches out to her father as his peer, accepts the bluntness with which he asserts his needs, and still maintains her own standards.

Then I noticed some of his behavior that started driving me crazy. For instance, after breakfast his flatulence would last for hours. Andre thought this was great fun. It smelled awful, but this goes with aging, so I didn't say anything. (Efficacy)

Efficacy requires realistic expectations about managing, rather than "mastering" or "resolving," personally challenging situations. It means asking others for help, while believing that in the end we are our own best resource.[8] Genevieve is able to avoid aggravating the situation by recognizing its realistic limitations. She can also consult with her pharmacist about her father's diet and supplements.

My father also got to me by clearing the condiments away from his plate, so that there was a clear swath the radius of his arm between his plate and anything else. Andre and I almost had everything in our laps as a result. I would replace the objects, and without raising his eyes he would move them again. And so it went through each meal. I knew this wouldn't change, so I tried to make a game of it. (Intrapersonal and Interpersonal Boundaries)

Permeable intrapersonal boundaries enhance the distinction between thinking and feeling, even while "clutched" with emotion. This enables reviewers to base decisions on the fleeting awareness of what is in their best interest and not simply on what decreases the intensity of their discomfort at the moment. So too, such boundaries enable them to stay committed to their convictions without needing to attack those of others.[9]

Functional interpersonal boundaries affect relationships, enabling reviewers to engage with others in goal-directed activity, to transcend self in intimacy, or to enjoy their solitude. These boundaries help reviewers to recover rapidly from stress and react less intensely to praise and criticism. They are guiding parameters for providing personal attention, physical support, and safety in care giving roles.[10] Permeable transpersonal boundaries enable reviewers to attend to the environment, to the universe, and to their life force.

Notice how Genevieve is able to manage eating meals together. Even though she is smarting over her father's long programmed table habits, she can see that his boundaries are closed to discussion about changing them. She makes the dynamics more acceptable for herself by responding to the absurdity of the scene with humor.

> *Accepting age old mannerisms is one thing, but making ends meet is something else. My father's contribution just wasn't enough for me to stretch my savings to cover our bills. So I spoke frankly with Andre, and told him the reasons I wanted him to be a go-between with his grandfather. One, I had made a deal that my father would determine the amount he helped, and now I wanted to change it. Two, he was extra generous to Andre. He'd give him five dollars each time Andre showed him his report card, even when the grades were nothing special. That afternoon Andre told my father how tight things were, and asked if he could increase his help by the amount I needed. To my surprise, my father said of course he would, and welled up as he said it. (Efficacy and Openness to Risk Taking)*

Openness to risk taking means living with uncertainty. When Genevieve agreed to let her father determine the extent to which he would help her financially, she took a chance that the household could make it. She had erred, and now needed to take an educated risk. This time *she* would ask for a specific amount, but through a mediator whom her father loved. The resolution occurs because the father wants to agree.

> *Andre and I had to collaborate on even more delicate matters. My father began losing the strength in his legs, and had to pull himself up the railing at night. Once he came down for the day, he was down. But our bathroom was upstairs, and I wanted some kind of commode that he could use downstairs. He was furious at the idea, and shouted, "I suppose you'll want to put diapers on me next!" Only later I found out he was using the bushes out back. (Openness to Risk Taking)*

Genevieve again erred by not anticipating and negotiating about this situation before the combined household began. She suggests a solution that her father refuses. She would have had to confront the issue more definitively if the following crisis had not occurred.

> *Then a special moment happened. My father was losing control over his bowels. He was so embarrassed that he would hide his underwear in his dresser. The smell was awful, and Andre hated it too. I used to remove the clothes and wash them, but now I had to act. That evening, my father soiled himself in my presence. I stayed cool, called for Andre, and asked him to fix a*

bath for his grandfather. In the bathroom he helped undress his grandfather, grabbed a towel and wiped him down. He drew a bath and helped him in, and for the next week was his nightly bath helper. Then, just as I was about to raise the commode matter again with my father, he was hospitalized for the endocarditis which killed him. (Interpersonal Boundary and Uniqueness)

Uniqueness rejects mechanisms of denial and projection, daring reviewers to own "all their thoughts, images, feelings, words, body, voice, actions, gestures, fantasies, and triumphs," and to recognize their negative thoughts and images as mere ideas that are not necessarily true.[11] In their place is the conviction that self is so much more than the sum of these parts and even more than their individuality. Acting on this conviction enabled the participants to avoid "adding insult to injury" as they respected one another's boundaries.

Andre and I have kept up a loving relationship over the years. I can live with his family any time I want, but I'm not ready yet. I'm still surviving by taking in paying borders. But that's another story altogether.

Self-esteem determines the quality of older adults' reminiscing. The mutually beneficial process of life review groups enables reviewers to appreciate that the "tumult" of their life is no less a source for the "mighty harmonies" filling their self-esteem.

Chapter Six

Embedded Shame

Mr. Duffy lived at a little distance from his body.—The Dubliners [1]

Older adults with hearty self-esteem are at one end of the continuum of self-esteem. At the other end are Mr. Duffy and many others who entered adulthood estranged from their very self. Theirs is an embedded shame transmitted over generations through toxic scripts and triangles. As children, they responded to insufficiently empathic caregivers by fusing shame and identity. Throughout life they have lived with the haunting assumption that they are "fundamentally defective, unworthy, not fully valid as a human being."[2]

TOXIC ISSUES

The frequency and intensity with which significant family members embroil specific children in toxic issues determine the prominence of shame in their lives. These issues, recurring over generations, prompt family members to react with excruciating anxiety, instead of coping with these issues when they arise. Fear that addressing these issues will impose lethal strains on members' health or family ties spurs kin to denial, projection, and somatic symptoms.

While family sensitivity can raise any issue to a level of toxicity, the most consistent issues include *wealth* (How much is enough? Who has access to it? How is it to be used?); *health* (use or avoidance of preventive and rehabilitative services; hypochondria; phobias); *sexuality* (adequate sex instruction; gender identity; infidelity; sexually transmitted diseases); *work* (workaholism; avoidance of work; product versus process orientation toward work); *anger* (forms of expression; targets); *religion* (freedom to choose; challenges to institutional tenets; fanaticism); and *autonomy* (What decisions are mine to make? Where can I live? How often am I expected to contact kin?)

Toxic issues are so many "islands of sensitivity" in a family. When family members even approach one of the islands, no more than a particular kind of look, a gesture, a word, or a tone of voice is needed to arouse an emotional explosion. One issue leads to the next and nothing is discussed to conclusion. Charges lead to countercharges, feelings mount, and chaos ensues.[3]

Heightened anxiety drives kin at this point to involve one another in any of three dysfunctional styles of interacting that further perpetuate these issues. First, family members may attempt to diminish anxiety by controlling one another's behavior related to the issues. Such efforts exacerbate the level of anxiety by eliciting defensive reactions from others trying to control their would-be-controllers.[4]

Second, participants may attempt to minimize anxiety by avoiding contact with the relatives involved in their toxic issues. Of course, lack of contact precludes a collaborative resolution of the issues, and encourages cutoffs which later generations may inherit.

TRIANGLES

The third reaction to the anxiety is the formation of triangles. When two family members feel that an issue threatens the relationship between them, they draw in a third to stabilize the original twosome. This third party may be an individual (child, spouse, or paramour); several people (in-laws, bowling team, supervisors); an object (beach house, racing car); or an issue (political affiliation, time away from the family).

In many triangles, one party is eventually perceived as a "persecutor," acting overtly in a manner that troubles the second party, an apparently innocent "victim." The third party intervenes between the other two as a "rescuer." In the end, however, the intervention neither helps the victim to take care of himself/herself/themselves, nor modifies the persecutor's behavior. Instead, it further locks the three parties into their triangulated positions, and diverts attention from the dyad's inability to work through the original toxic issue.

A triangle requires the active cooperation of all its members. Each party's attention to the actions of the others, however, discounts his/her/their contribution to the maintenance of the triangle. This myopia leads the members to blame one another, rather than to accept responsibility for maintaining their own dysfunctional roles.

A husband, for instance, who is reluctant to respond to his wife's needs, can foster an over-involved relationship between his wife and daughter. The wife, in turn, can accept the compensatory gratification from this relationship rather than confront her feelings of abandonment when her husband withdraws. The daughter, too, finds benefits in this arrangement. She may have privileges inappropriate to her age or enjoy being an intimate companion to her mother.

Triangles may have different configurations depending upon the specific issue which precipitates their formation. A father may "persecute" a daughter when the issue involves her social life, yet also be "the victim" of her refusal to accept a position in the family business. However, once family members have committed themselves to a position around a specific toxic issue in their family of origin, they tend to keep this same position whenever that issue arises in other emotionally charged relationships, e.g., with their spouse, children, in-laws, friends, or colleagues.

Other siblings who are more lightly embroiled in fewer triangles have higher levels of self-esteem. It is important to note when siblings at any level enter intimate relationships, they do so with partners who are at levels similar to their own. So there are ongoing differences in the self-esteem-through-shame continuum in the following generations both among siblings and cousins. Without clinical intervention these differences can continue indefinitely.

EMBEDDED SHAME AS TORMENT

In a reflex motion embedded shame confounds cognitive functioning as it constricts the diaphragm, binds the tongue, accelerates blushing and heart rate, and freezes spontaneous movement.[5] It drives its hosts to avert their eyes, stoop their spine, tense their muscles, and gesticulate awkwardly.[6] Such physical demeanor reveals the dread of having failed profoundly as a person.

Triggering events are everywhere: simple awareness of limitations and failures, an intimacy rebuffed, a critical remark from a friend. Suddenly, shame feelings and thoughts surge together, amplifying each other until they engulf the self. Sartre described the condition as "an immediate shudder which runs through me from head to foot without any discursive preparation."[7] The bearers of such acutely painful experiences only want them to end quickly, and have little desire to reflect upon them.[8]

BYPASSING SHAME

Flight from shame, however, only compounds distress by burying shame beneath feelings less painful to bear. Substituting guilt in place of shame feels less burdensome because guilt focuses upon the act done or not done, while shame is about the self. Some use anger to bypass shame. Anger does not rectify faux pas, but it helps the perpetrators to dissociate themselves from blame.[9] Of course, when shame bearers feel anger toward someone they love, they may block awareness of their anger and direct it back upon the self as depression.[10] In fact, since depression can feel comparatively acceptable when compared with acute shame, shame bearers often substitute it whenever their anxiety mounts about some defeat, defect, or disgrace.[11]

WOUNDED VISIBILITY

The hallmark of shame is an obsession with being exposed "to the immediate evaluation of others, and a general readiness to believe that these evaluations are more negative than they really are."[12] This preoccupation raises blame protection to the primary consideration in decision making, and amplifies any degree of criticism to a global indictment. Exaggerated self-criticism can sever shame bearers, as with Mr. Duffy, even from themselves.

Accordingly, many live as though concealing their felt defectiveness through a rigidly controlled presentation of self, reaction-formation, and dissembling can compensate for self-acceptance and spontaneous behavior. Shame bearers become experienced at picking up others' cues and trying to control relationships by pleasing, apologizing, or seldom disagreeing. They sacrifice intimacy for harmony and predictability.[13]

They are anxious, for example, that an unguarded expression might convey hostility. When they hear themselves make a surprisingly sarcastic remark, they feel once again caught unaware, exposed. They self-consciously scan their motives and behavior, "unable fully to engage the self in any activity requiring that the greater part of attention be directed away from the image of the self."[14] They may even conceal their fear by "acting as a computer, very correct, very reasonable with no semblance of any feeling showing."[15]

Shame bearers do not trust others to respect them, and their dread of public exposure estranges them from mutually caring interaction. They receive praise as patronizing and criticism as confirming some vast discrepancy between their aspirations and their abilities. This estrangement also skews their spirituality by focusing exclusively upon their supposed existential unworthiness. Since religious shame bearers are concerned that God not find them wanting even in the minutiae of their lives, they are wary of their God as well.

Not surprisingly, their obsession with expected hostility often leads to a "shame rage" rejecting the rejecters. The rage protects them from feeling inferior by projecting upon others responsibility for their discomfort. In short, "I have no reason to be ashamed; the problem starts with the others who are attacking me."

Complicating rage further, shame bearers may process their retaliation as illogical because others have only acted as the shamed deserve. Moreover, their rage can antagonize others for whom they genuinely care, and thus isolate them more thoroughly. To manage this dilemma, some direct rage inward as depression. Others try to gain power, admiration or intellectual superiority, and often engage in downward social comparisons.[16]

Cornelius

Cornelius is a seventy-one year old retired high school principal who recalled a childhood incident with many hallmarks of embedded shame. He was his parents' "fair haired boy," an only son with two sisters. Even in the children's presence the parents would brag about them, describing them as "two angels and an archangel." For Cornelius, however, the honorific meant that he needed to surpass his sisters' accomplishments, to show that he merited the higher ranking.

His parents compounded this dynamic by settling Cornelius in a volatile triangle. His father demanded that family members write a note each time they left the house that gave the reason for leaving the premises. At day's end his father read the notes.

My mother accepted this because she shopped a lot, and did as she pleased so long as she left her note. But when my father thought she was spending too much, my parents would argue until my mother ended up smashing the dinner plates in the sink. I'd get so upset that I would hurry from my room where I was doing homework to comfort her. She'd be alone in the kitchen sobbing. We'd hug each other, and she'd pat my head until we both calmed down.

To help my mother feel happier, I made sure to tell her whenever I got really good grades. My fourth grade teacher held a weekly spelling bee, and often I was the only boy who made it to the final round. What I didn't tell her was that during the bee my teeth would chatter and my thumb would flinch with nervousness. Then, one morning I went through all this grief, but didn't make the final round.

That afternoon a few kids at a time left class to have their scalps examined, because the school had an infestation of lice. During my examination, a member of the health care team from the city's board of education asked how I liked school. I told him, "I hate it and all its stupid tests!" The following day, the teacher again sent me to the examination room, and there was my mother! She had not told me that the health care team had contacted her about my comments. I immediately felt responsible for the wounded, mortified look on her face. The team member reminded me about my answer the day before, and asked me to tell them more about it so my mother could know too. I stammered something, but decided that the truth would make matters worse. Without looking at my mother I played down yesterday's remarks, and added that I liked some subjects better than others, especially when I could diagram sentences. Then I was sent back to class.

That evening my mother explained, "When strangers ask a personal question, you do not have to tell them all about yourself. You can be vague. After all, we don't need to make ourselves look bad." But I had made my mom look bad. I was desolate. I had failed already, and I was only in the fourth grade. I was determined it wouldn't happen again. So I've "faked it" a lot. I scan the environment. I watch my words. And I never exceed my level of competence. Let someone else mess up being superintendant of the school system. I've managed fine enough as a principal.

The ongoing family triangle had compromised Cornelius's level of self-esteem early on. Even by the fourth grade misplaced responsibility for his mother's happiness made the episode above traumatic for him. His response to his mother's lecture set his life long trajectory to lower his aspirations instead of seeking self-fulfillment. He is also "managing fine enough" in the life review group because he determines what he chooses to share, and receives encouragement from the facilitator and colleagues.

When shame distances older adults from themselves, it does not at all improve their perspective.

Chapter Seven

Paradox

Be patient toward all that is unresolved in your heart. . . . Try to love the contradictions themselves. . . . Do not now seek resolutions, which cannot be given because you would not be able to live them, and the point is to live everything. Live the contradictions now. Perhaps you will then gradually, without noticing it, live along some distant day into the resolutions.—When Silence Reigns[1]

This chapter explains how a paradoxical perspective about reminiscences can so optimize the reviewers' lens of self-esteem that they discover self-acceptance in these very memories. Facilitators typically introduce paradox only after members have shared their initial reminiscences and the group has grown cohesive. Their orientation includes a gentle summary of content about family systems, its impact on self-esteem, and the latter's role in influencing reviewers' capacity to accept memories compassionately. Referring mainly, though not exclusively, to verbal paradoxes, they then segue to the success of paradoxes in disclosing unattended, more inclusive perspectives for reviewing personal history.

Paradoxes stimulate a creative tension by seeking *both-and* answers to *either-or* dilemmas. As contradictions, paradoxes initially frustrate reasoning-to-understand. Paradoxes are self-contradictory statements that arise from incongruent viewpoints, e.g., Groucho Marx's observation that "the keys to success in business are honesty and fair dealing. If you can fake them both, you've got it made." For those, however, who can stay with "the tension of opposites that are held simultaneously," paradoxes will evoke syntheses that transcend the contradictions.[2]

The following four chapters present paradoxes chosen because they have been particularly fruitful in empowering older adults to stretch the limits on self-esteem that their self-development has imposed. Paradoxes found in poetry, show tunes, and the reviewers' own wordplay can neutralize the hazards to life review arising from the epigenetic self. Similarly, the paradoxical approach of extending one's own life review to include five generations can correct the distortions inherent in the toxic issues and triangles of the family scripted self. The paradoxes of Mystical Night and Engaged Detachment successfully access the metaphysical self. Consider the paradoxes in Victoria's life review.

Victoria

Victoria is a seventy-nine year old house keeper and the youngest of three sisters. She had initially questioned whether she ever had an identity because she appeared almost invisible in her memories. She recalled that when the sisters were in their twenties, the extended family applauded her oldest sister's glamour, the next sister's ambition to illustrate children's books, and relegated Victoria to the afterthought of caring for the household. Over the decades as she hosted extended family gatherings, guests would greet her, thank her, and kiss her goodbye without otherwise speaking with her at any length.

The week after Victoria learned about the power of paradox, she attended the next session of her group with a book her nephew brought home from college. She shared with her colleagues a paradox that her nephew had been telling his relatives:

> *Quoting from the book I have here about quantum physics, he read that "all being at the sub-atomic level can be described equally well either as solid particles, like so many minute billiard balls, or as waves, like undulations of the surface of the sea."[3] He went on about this phenomenon with us, and told us that over eons a synthesis may have evolved from this tension among quanta to form our human consciousness. He read some more, "Unless consciousness is something that just suddenly emerges . . . then it was there in some form all along as a basic property of the constituents of all matter."[4] Wow!*
>
> *Since both our last meeting and my nephew's book were about paradoxes, I decided to look at myself through a paradox. From one angle, my place in the family guaranteed that I'd grow up discounted. I have nieces, cousins, an aunt, and two great-grandmothers who were given the left over family roles because they were the youngest females. For years I wished that I had been born in a safer position or been a man. But from another angle, those were not the choices for me. The only choice was whether I wanted to exist or not. 'Cause if I changed anything in my history, I would be eliminating me! I'd be a different person. NO, no! Whatever bad breaks I've had, I want to be me.*

Similar to Victoria's experience, paradox can enable reviewers to acknowledge that formative components of their identity reside in relationships that also transmitted shame and sustained it throughout a lifetime. Now, however, instead of repeating their history of rationalizing, denying, or protesting against these relationships, they can accept and use their shame-inducing history as a quixotic component of self-acceptance. They can appreciate how shame became entwined in "how I do me," and now affirm their identity as "good enough." Victoria even acknowledged that her invisibility had freed her to indulge in her private, gratifying world of reading. For the volume she carried to our session was her own newly purchased copy.

APPLYING PARADOX

Group members usually find paradoxes in two ways. In the first, they search easily accessible, popular sources. Facilitators often gather such sources for them, e.g., period music scores, decades-old *New York Times* front pages, anthologies of poems, books of children's rhymes, and the plays of Shakespeare and Gilbert and Sullivan. Reviewers apply the paradoxes to specific memories they have trouble accepting as part of their personal history.

In the second, facilitators present their groups with a generous list of paradoxes which members then match to memories that the list invariably, often unexpectedly, evokes. Such a list may include such taunting examples of paradoxical wordplay as:

- the substitution of one part of speech for another, e.g., "he sang his didn't and danced his did." (e.e. cummings)[5]
- words that mean one thing and also the opposite, e.g., "I really *buckled* down when I studied for the written component of my driver's test. Then I *buckled* altogether when I hit the curbs each time I tried the three corner turn."
- the seemingly inappropriate substitution of one word for another because there is no definable relationship between the two, e.g., "We burn daylight," and "O benefit of ill." (Shakespeare)[6]
- words that sound alike but differ in meaning (homonyms) and words that sound alike but differ in spelling and meaning (homophones), e.g., "What's the *point* of all this remembering? The memories keep *pointing* to the mess I've made of things. Still, I'm hoping these paradoxes can help me see that all-in-all my contributions total a *point* or two more than my short comings."
- inconsistent explanations, e.g., "It is only by effort that a man achieves the inevitable." (Justice Oliver Wendell Holmes); Thomas Jefferson "had the deep deviousness that is given only to the pure of heart;"[7] the confounding

advice offered to an ambitious French peasant, "If you were a fool, you might let yourself be taken in by them [exaggerated compliments]; if you want to succeed, you *must* let yourself be taken in by them."[8]

• the juxtaposition of seemingly contradictory words (oxymorons), e.g., "Every Frenchman wants to benefit from one or several privileges. It is his way of affirming his passion for equality." (Charles de Gaulle); his friend had not "a single redeeming vice." (Oscar Wilde)[9]

PARADOX'S COGNITIVE ENTRAPMENT

A group's supportive give-and-take helps reviewers to stay with their ruminations about the conundrum until a resolution breaks through. In Rilke's words, the group encourages members "to love the contradictions" and "live the contradictions now." For this initial tension keeps mounting until it precipitates its resolution.

Sophie, for instance, recalled scenes from over several decades in which she addressed her behavior in absolute terms, i.e., she was either *In or Out*; her decisions were either *Black or White*; her responses *Hot or Cold*. These reminiscences tormented her because she seldom measured up to the standards involved and others never did. Sophie is sixty-eight, and had recently returned from a tour of Ireland where she was celebrating her retirement. Her colleagues in the life review group inquired whether her tour had provided any paradoxes relevant to her memories. With only a pause, she recalled that their bus driver stopped occasionally at pubs so that the passengers could use the facilities. Intrigued that the driver had straddled a double yellow line when parking the bus, she played at entrapping him in a misdemeanor. Sophie asked him about the meaning of a single yellow line bordering the far side of the road. His reply, "It means you can't park there at all." She then asked for the meaning of the double yellow line beneath the bus. His reply was simply, "O that means you can't park here at all, at all!"

"Here was the resolution to a *living* paradox," Sophie chuckled, continuing her insight:

> The driver, of course, knew the rules, and exempted himself to park where his experience taught him it was a convenient and safe location for us passengers. Prudent adults draw on their intelligence to guide them in following rules. I'm hoping that I can be more mellow in handling the yellow lines ahead for me.

Sophie's level of self-esteem enabled her to appreciate how her scheme for entrapping the driver reflected primarily on her own rigidity. The driver's humor nudged her to ease into her own "efforts at relaxing."

RESOLVING PARADOX

Sophie's insight, like all syntheses that emerge from joined contradictions, offers an aerial, inclusive perspective for reviewing memories. It is the fruit, in Rilke's words, of trying "to love the contradictions themselves without seeking resolutions," without forcing them. Once the cognitive tension releases its resolution, however, this new disarming perspective enables reviewers to appreciate the significance of details previously overlooked or taken for granted, such as,

- the tenacity of toxic issues over the generations
- extenuating circumstances surrounding decisions
- ambiguity about the meaning of people's intent and behavior
- the positive connotations of events, e.g., interpreting mistakes as "needed feedback," another's nagging as "interest and caring," and symptoms as "signaling devices" to reach out for needed resources.

Drawing upon G.K. Chesterton's epigram that "the essence of every picture is the frame," this new perspective *reframes* their reminiscences.[10] Even though the events and relationships recalled remain unaltered, the change in perspective alters their meaning and mood, and makes it possible to recast unfortunate experiences as essential and valuable. This reframing of reminiscences then enables reviewers to turn the corrective lens of paradox upon their own self-assessment.

Josef

One older alcoholic, for instance, about to try A.A. again after "too many times to count" reframed her self-assessment in these terms, "Dr. King spoke about the redemptive value of unmerited suffering; now I'm looking into the value of *merited* suffering." Another life review member concluded that she and her colleagues were "remembering a different future," i.e., opening opportunities for constructive behavior in the future through compassionate acceptance of their past right now.

Josef, a seventy-two year old retired ophthalmologist, questioned whether his life review is a resource in planning for his future, or a script depicting how he would recycle shame. He reported how his father, a dermatologist, had taught him to get ahead *by always being "in the driver's seat,"* claiming the right of way, and deriding others who did not belong in the fast lane.

I passed my father only to become my father writ large! What's more, I've resented red lights all my life and never relaxed enough to enjoy my traveling. I'm trying to apply to myself the paradox a sage gave to his disciple, "You are on a journey without distance; to stop is to arrive."

So now I've begun to stop at real traffic lights whenever they even begin to change. In my retirement-bound RV, this scruple can be my courtesy to others and a gift to myself. At each red light perhaps I can savor the trip as well as the destination because doing so is not my style. In my RV maybe I can be a little less "driven."

Josef understood that he would recycle his driven behavior at times *and,* nonetheless, have the behavior be more his own and less his father's.

Samila

Eighty year old Samila also presented an issue that had been toxic for her. She recalled her principal challenge as a young adult:

As the only daughter, I had to choose between loyalty to my family and marrying the person I loved. My family folklore included tales of many relatives coming down hard on "defectors," and my own situation was no less intense. My mother's father, who lived with us, announced that if I became engaged to my boyfriend, he would take to his bed and stop eating. When I protested to my parents that his behavior was unfair to me, they simply replied, "You know how he is." Later they objected that they would be party to his death, if they approved my engagement. So I moved out, and my grandfather died from malnutrition. Then, my fiancé broke off our engagement three weeks before the wedding. When I contacted my parents, they told me I was no longer family to them. You know, over the years rather than infuriating me, their rejection's confirmed a guilt I cannot shake.

Group members spoke from their hearts about the debilitating sequence of losses Samila had endured, "Your grandfather destroyed your peace of mind. You left behind your home. Your fiancé deserted you. Your parents rejected you. Anyone would be devastated!" Finally, one colleague proposed a paradox for this reminiscence. A fancier of poetry, he recited lines that contrasted the sense of loss and loneliness associated with death with the merriment of a tavern,

"And may we find when ended is the page
Death but a tavern on our pilgrimage."[11]

He encouraged Samila "to loiter at the bar," attentive to the stories of fellow pilgrims and sharing her own reflections about her memories.

The following week Samila responded:

In the scene you quoted death is not the end; death is an occasion for fellowship. We are fellow pilgrims to one another on our life course. Your stories have moved me to reach out to my cousins who have not involved me in their lives out of respect for my parents. I'm going to contact them, and invite them into mine. And, while I'm at it, I am bringing my knitting skills to the senior center to join the group making afghans for homeless newborns. This page may be ending, but there's a whole other chapter to come.

In the closing sessions of their life review groups, facilitators encouraged Sophie, Josef, Samila, and all the other participants using paradoxes to give some criteria for measuring their impact. Their replies included improvements in:

- basing my decisions on what is really in my best interest, and not on some quick-fix to calm my feelings for a while.
- accepting things about myself that I'm ashamed of, without blaming others.
- seeing myself realistically instead of strutting myself and insulting others.
- informing my own opinions and problem management plans instead of conforming to others' expectations.
- expressing my feelings more directly instead of monitoring my own spontaneous behavior.

These reviewers have succinctly blended life review and self-esteem.

Older adults can draw upon a limitless number of paradoxes. These paradoxes can enable reviewers to "be patient toward all that is unresolved" in their heart, because the day is here to live the contradictions "into the resolutions."

Chapter Eight

Poetic Paradox

last night
the fears of my mother came
knocking and when i
opened the door
they tried to explain themselves
and I understood
everything they said.—Breaklight[1]

After introducing life review participants to the power of paradox, facilitators ease them into discovering paradoxes by distributing anthologies of poems.[2] Members select poems which express themes that are prominent in their lives and include paradoxical imagery corresponding to these themes. Most participants find that poetry is an inexhaustible resource that revives significant memories, captures the emotional tone of scenes from their past, and expresses the meaning that these scenes now hold for them.

The excerpt above from Lucille Clifton is a concise example of poetic paradox. The fears of the mother have become a toxic theme because the narrator too has barred them from consciousness. "Last night," however, the narrator finally does "open the door" to dream about her mother's fears. The narrator's "understanding everything" confirms the paradox that releasing fears requires bearing and withstanding the dread of "opening the door."

Participants report that they have little difficulty in finding poems with paradoxes. They begin with verses from the works of their favorite bard, or selected from poems treating a treasured subject, such as nature's beauty, marital and parental ties, or perseverance in adversity. Moreover, those who are more familiar with poetry in a language other than English are in the empowering position of introducing colleagues to the literature of their own culture.

47

THE POWER OF POETIC PARADOX[3]

Embedded in the attractiveness of poetry, paradox challenges errant perspectives from which reviewers may be assessing their reminiscences. Paradox presents a contradiction that reviewers cannot resolve so long as they cling to the circularity of viewing themselves through the lens of their own distorted self-esteem. Poetry is a prompt, moving older adults to entertain new, affirming insights about themselves. When they share these insights in the group, other members can also validate them.

Celeste

Celeste suffers from arthritis in her lower spine that has recurred twice after surgeries, and continues to limit her mobility profoundly. Widowed and alienated from her children, she is now seventy-two years old, the reverse (27) of her mother's age at the time she died. This numerical connection had reminded her of the unusual lines with which her mother had soothed Celeste at bedtime,

> *Lie there quiet, calm as the tomb.*
> *For rest will pass by much too soon,*
> *And sorrow join you by your bed.*

Ironically her mother's song tried to comfort her with what seemed to be prophetic references to her mother's own death and to Celeste's current suffering. During the past week, however, Celeste came upon these lines from William Blake,

> *Sleep, sleep, happy child,*
> *All creation slept and smil'd;*
> *Sleep, sleep, happy sleep,*
> *While o'er thee thy mother weep.*[4]

The overlay of the two songs helped me understand that my mother would certainly weep if she knew I had concluded that aging means only sorrow. I can't deny my pain, so I mean to draw some good from it. I'm beginning by reaching out to my children. Look, I've even brought a lock of my mother's hair to show you. I've always cherished it, and now it's a sign of my hope that the hearts of all three generations will be free from suffering.

Celeste recognizes that relieving the sorrow in her own life is an opportunity after the fact to staunch her mother's sorrow. Her mother's hair becomes a talisman that Celeste's outreach to her children can renew the future.

Gertrude

Eighty-two year old Gertrude, who had grown up at a terminal city on the Erie Canal, punned upon the lock of hair to add her own insight into Celeste's reminiscence:

> *You hold a* lock *and a* lock *holds you. Your surgeries and troubled family ties have been so many gates raising the water level in the* life lock *you are passing through. They enable you to travel beyond the rivers and canals of earlier stages to the "Great Lakes" of this current stage in your life. This* life lock *and* hair lock *both provide continuity with your past, and open to more adventures ahead.*

Delia

Delia is eighty-one years old, the primary care giver for her disabled husband for seven years. Her colleagues noted that she usually spoke more about meeting her husband's needs than her own, when she shared her reminiscences. She replied that her family would never approve of her "complaining."

> *My family motto, "If you fall, don't stop to rise," captures the urgency that my family puts on coping with whatever situation comes your way. If the going is rough, then "show what we're made of." In fact, our premise seems to be that the worse the discomfort, the higher the level of achievement we'll reach when we persevere.*

Her colleagues pointed out, however, that the tension in this process would never end, since solutions to earlier problems can become new problems, and know-how can eventually become obsolete. They added that the idea of an anxiety-achievement ratio seemed to be a particularly masochistic method of predicting progress.

Their comments moved Delia to say,

> *I've often felt that I was under pressure without a corresponding "payoff." For years I worked in my husband's picture frame shop. Then, one year I added babysitting my granddaughter, caring for my terminally ill father, and attending to my mother's clinical despondency. I'm beginning to see how my self-denial was tantamount to denying that I even had a self. But now I'm trying to temper my mood by calmly reciting from The Hound of Heaven each morning:*
>
>> *Is my gloom, after all,*
>> *Shade of His hand outstretched caressingly?*[5]

To be honest, I know that over the decades I really have managed again and again to cope with new crises, but the difference between the pressure I'm under and the satisfaction I get from my modest accomplishments is disheartening. Still, I do know my mood is a "caress." I acclaim it so each time I sing our anthem, Lift Every Voice and Sing:

> *Shadowed beneath Thy hand,*
> *May we forever stand.*[6]

At our next session Delia shared a resolve she made after reading this excerpt from William Wordsworth's *The Tables Turned:*

> *Our meddling intellect*
> *Misshapes the beauteous forms of things;*
> *We murder to dissect . . . .*
> *Come forth, and bring with you a heart*
> *That watches and receives.*[7]

I can see where I "butchered" our family motto in my hurried, self-effacing rescuing of others. I mean to "watch and receive" as well every day, and I know I'll have to begin to ask in order to receive.

Ironically it takes the raw metaphor of "murdering" to alert Delia that the conclusions she draws from her familial programming "misshape the beauteous," comforting theme of the poems she has chosen. Awakened, she means to love others just as she loves herself.

Walter

Walter, a seventy-eight year old retired fire chief, shared reminiscences that emphasized the theme of relentless self-improvement. He reported, for instance:

Growing up in my family was a mixed bag. My parents were on my case a lot to be tops at school, but I also enjoyed that limelight when I succeeded. One time I told my father, "I can't do this," when I brought him a grammar school assignment. He corrected me, "'Can't' is not in this family's vocabulary." Then, when I was entering high school, my parents purchased an oversized china closet to hold the scholarship and forensic trophies they expected me to win. To my cousins' chagrin, they went on about my achievements at every wake and wedding.

    Probably I was just "cutting off my nose to spite my face," but I seized up under my parents' pressure to complete a swath of college applications. I told them I needed a break from school, and sullenly refused to apply for college. When my parents insisted I would have to pay rent until I returned to school, I joined the fire department. But when my parents died a decade later I returned

*to college in the evening, and over the years passed a series of civil service
exams that promoted me to chief. I recall my wife referring to herself as an
"exam widow" whose children had an "absentee father."*

Recognizing that his achievements were ever further behind him, Walter
chose William Blake's *Eternity* for the paradox which epitomized his
dilemma:

> *He who binds to himself a joy*
> *Does the winged life destroy;*
> *But he who kisses the joy as it flies*
> *Lives in eternity's sun rise.*[8]

He explained,

> *I've been unable to "kiss joy 'Hello' or 'Good Bye'" because I've been trying
> to "bind" joys to myself with all those trophies and promotions. Now I see how
> I've sacrificed relationships to my ambition, and it all seems irredeemable to
> me.*

A colleague intervened to guide him beyond this impasse. She urged Walter
to reflect on the paradox she had selected from Alexander Pope's *The Dying
Christian to His Soul*. For her it succeeded in reframing "either-or" choices
as "both-and":

> *Vital spark of heav'nly flame!*
> *Quit, oh quit this mortal frame;*
> *Trembling, hoping, ling'ring, flying,*
> *Oh the pain, the bliss of dying!*
> *Cease, fond Nature, cease thy strife,*
> *And let me languish into life.*[9]

Walter appreciated the poem's honesty concerning the unavoidable
ambivalence about dying, and seized upon the image of "languishing into
life" to describe a new course his marital and parental relationships could
pursue. He proposed that one path open to him now was talking candidly
with his family, one on one. He would apologize, and ask them to invite him
into their lives.

At the following session, Walter described the heartening conversation he
had broached with his wife, and ended with a paradox that echoed Blake's.
From William Shakespeare's *That Time of Year Thou Mayst in Me Behold*,
he read,

> *In me thou see'st the twilight of such day*
> *As after sunset fadeth in the west, . . .*
> *This thou perceiv'st, which makes thy love more strong,*
> *To love that well which thou must leave ere long.*

He concluded, "I'm finally ready to start at some reaching out, and love those well whom I 'must leave ere long.'" Notice how the affirming tone of "languishing into life" and making "thy love more strong" both forestalls regret and accentuates the satisfaction of feeling "At Last!" Walter is, indeed, indebted to his colleague in the group.

Darlene

Darlene is a seventy-seven year old retired librarian, the first born of six children. Her reminiscences showed her assuming responsibilities as though they justified her existence. For instance, when Darlene learned the family folklore that her mother had lost fourteen pounds during the first eight months of her pregnancy with her, she determined to make it up to her mother in dutifulness. To illustrate this, she read the group a letter she wrote to her mother when she was seven:

> *I know a lot of things about this world. It took me a long time to know about them. So now I know what I shall be when I grow up. I shall be a hard work lady. If you are alive then you will get part of my money of course.*

Darlene commuted to college in order to hold a job in her home town and defray her parents' expenses. While raising her own family, she also became the primary caregiver for her widowed, infirm mother. Now she was bereft that her four children lived out of state. She visited each child's family for two weeks twice a year, even though arguments between her children and grandchildren upset her considerably. She chose her paradox from Shelley's *Ode to the West Wind:*

> *Oh, lift me as a wave, a leaf, a cloud!*
> *I fall upon the thorns of life! I bleed!*
> *A heavy weight of hours has chain'd and bow'd*
> *One too like thee: tameless, and swift, and proud.*[10]

She continued:

> *I've yearned to be "tameless," but I only feel good enough when I've "borne the heavy weight" of responsibilities. But now I'm feeling an exhaustion that's moving me to reconsider my life course. I want to accept myself even when I feel unworthy. I'm entitled to accept myself; I don't have to earn it. But I seem to have summed up my whole life in my childhood letter, and now I'm probably settling for exhaustion in lieu of calm.*

A colleague responded by urging Darlene to consider Edith Lovejoy Pierce's *Thou Art Within Me Like a Sea* which he then read to the group:

> *Thou art within me like a sea,*
> *Filling me as a slowly rising tide,*

Thou art within me like a sea at dawn.[11]

This imagery initially confounded Darlene in two ways. On the one hand, she could feel herself drowning at dawn as the tide of responsibility engulfed her. On the other hand, she is drowning even now because, as inevitably as the tide itself, she cannot escape feeling unworthy unless she is submerged with tasks. "What a loss," he added, "that you cannot appreciate the rising tide, instead, as filling channels for your delight and raising surf for your relaxation!"

Then, at the next session Darlene replied that although her feelings were "stuck,"

> *hopefully I can act more freely by owning my "programming." How could I have lived as I did all these decades and not be as I am? A tide of self-acceptance is coming in- even if I still find the water on the chilly side.*

She ended her remarks delighting in a newly found poetic paradox taken from T. B. Aldrich's *Lycidas:*

> *"I hope," said Lycidas, "for peace at last;*
> *I only ask for peace! my God is Ease:*
> *Day after day some rude iconoclast*
> *Breaks all my images."*[12]

"My image captioned 'duty bound' may be the last to break," she mused, "but I can already see some cracks in it!" The poetry has sensitized Darlene to that law of gradualness: modifying driven behavior follows its own timetable.

Daniel

Daniel is a retired dentist, eighty-four years old. His life review had evoked a skein of reminiscences about his life-long commitment to civil rights. He recalled the challenges in creating dental clinics for migrant workers, mentoring minority interns, and later accepting Medicaid patients others had turned away. He focused, though, on the superiority he had felt because of his "selfless" character rather than on his egalitarian commitment. He was despondent over recalling so vividly his ledger of hidden satisfaction in being more honorable than those who had not taken the risks he did. He felt rotten from the inside out.

In a month's time he found relevant paradoxes in three Shakespearean plays. He shared each, in turn, followed by his own commentary: *"Every man has a fault, and honesty is his"* (*Timon of Athens*, Act 3, Scene 1). Daniel pointed out that it was not honesty but pride that was his fault. He claimed for himself the paradoxical description about Julius Caesar's conceitedness: *"But when I tell him he hates flatterers, He says he does, being then most flattered"* (*Julius Caesar*, Act 2, Scene 1). He saw the same "tawdry conceitedness" of his own motives negating the value of his work. He was a contradiction: *"The trumpet of his own virtues . . . "* (*Much Ado About Nothing*, Act 5, Scene 2).

When he had finished, his colleagues joined in a spirited discussion which noted the severe and emotionally laden language Daniel used about himself. A colleague also observed that Daniel had erred in identifying his "fault" because his fault was, indeed, "honesty." He was so focused on being honest in his self-assessment that he had developed tunnel vision. Concern about the purity of his intentions was preventing him from accepting the reality that multiple motives over-determine everyone's behavior.

At the following session, Daniel was able to use the insight about his misuse of honesty to transcend the paradox. "O.K., I've got it! I may have done the better deed, but still that does not mean that I am better than anyone else!" The tone of his life review became lighter as he incorporated recollections of many other gratifying roles in addition to his dental career and his participation in civil rights. When other participants held the floor in their turn, he was attentive to their presentations and open to their experiences because he had become more accepting of his own.

Roxanne

Roxanne is a potter, an eighty-three year old single woman who had supported herself by selling her fine crockery at fairs along the East coast. Her compulsive management of time enabled her to hide her poor self-esteem beneath a prodigious volume of work. She rigidly scheduled her time, and felt agitated whenever she was interrupted. This discomfort permeated her life review as well. Roxanne repeatedly compared her reputation and productivity to the artistic success of her grandparents and great aunts and uncles in Europe.

An indeterminate sense of loss permeated her life review. As the source for her paradoxes she too had chosen Shakespeare: *"Let us not burden our remembrances with a heaviness that's gone"* (*The Tempest*, Act 5, Scene 1).

Roxanne explained that she had long since established her reputation. Her scrap book bulged with awards and testimonials. She had no need to prove herself, to measure her creativity and execution against anyone else's. She had the opportunity now to work for her own delight, and yet she burdened herself with the same pressure that confronted neophytes. Driven and edgy, she sighed that her own attitude precluded her from enjoying her own talents. "I am like Penelope who spun wool during the decade of her husband's odyssey," she said, and quoted: *"All the yarn she spun in Ulysses' absence did but fill Ithaca full of moths"* (*Coriolanus*, Act I, Scene 3).

During the ensuing week, memories of her parents' fervid expectations for her artistic career heightened her anger about her inability to delight in her work for its own sake.

> *My parents exalted their own parents and kin as role models for me. Instead of whetting my talents, though, they were priming me to exceed their accomplishments, as though there were literal truth in the paradox: "We burn daylight" (Romeo and Juliet, Act 1, Scene 4).*

A colleague observed that Roxanne had not included her parents among the artists in the family. She explained that both were eldest children who had left school prematurely to supplement their fathers' incomes. Their siblings as adults acknowledged this sacrifice, and were eager to encourage their niece's career. The entire family, she saw, was trying to compensate for the surrender of her parents' talents. Her career had evolved circuitously out of her grandparents' poverty and fecundity.

The following week she read a line from Shakespeare:

> *"O benefit of ill" (Sonnet 119). This line has played out over the generations in the fruitfulness of my own career. Now I'm planning to recycle this "benefit" once more. I'm going to use the energy that's fueled my competitiveness to conduct creative workshops at our senior center.*

A knowledgeable group member commented simply, "I hear Generativity talking!" For, Roxanne intended to exploit her competitiveness for the artistic development of others. Indeed, to borrow from Lucille Clifton, as Roxanne's memories "tried to explain themselves," she now "understood everything they said."

Chapter Nine

Word Play as Paradox

And we are put on earth a little space, That we may learn to bear the beams of love.—The Little Black Boy [1]

Older adults particularly enjoy converting two kinds of word play to paradoxes for reframing their life review. These sources for paradoxes are the metaphors in lyrics and the homonyms and homophones with which they convey their own memories.

METAPHORS

The songs are the initial attraction for group members. Even as a facilitator is showing the song books and recordings for a group's use in discovering metaphors, participants begin singing their favorite songs, or humming them when they forget the lyrics. Only after they have recalled the singers famous for recording the songs and the shows in which the songs appeared and them, do the reviewers move on to the metaphors themselves.

Metaphors are comparisons that communicate insights by transferring the literal meaning of a word to a different category with which it shares certain characteristics, e.g., "Watch me *outfox* my crooked landlord." The example expresses a connection between incongruous categories (human tenant-resourceful animal). By setting the familiar in an unfamiliar context and juxtaposing words and images, metaphors prompt users to interpret their ordinary world in extraordinary terms.

This combination of familiar and unfamiliar features or the unfamiliar combination of familiar features permeates daily speech, e.g., a wooden face, starry-eyed, a crenellated brow, horsing around, foot of a mountain, eye of a needle. Facilitators point out examples that group members have been interjecting into their conversations and recollections, and encourage their groups to point out metaphors in one another's speech. For instance, in response to the recollection, "When I finally stood up to the bully, I felt as bold as a lion," colleagues would point to this imagery as an example of metaphor.

This metaphor becomes paradoxical once a facilitator or colleague asks, "What other characteristics of a lion besides 'boldnes' appear in your reminiscences? The question challenges the reviewer by proposing that an *unintended* characteristic of the object referred to (the lion) can be the key in opening new perspectives about themes and scenes under review. The reviewer's staying power in following the free association after that exchange evokes the recognition, the "aha!" experience, of new insight into memories. Free association, of course, does not occur freely. Wants, fears, and goals over-determine the emergent content of thought.

A reviewer's speculation, for example, might focus on the way in which lions hunt, and see some similarities to his earlier relationships with his sisters. Like the male lion who eats the prey the lionesses hunt down, he may recall how he connived to have his sisters do his chores and bake brownies for his friends. Then he may remember how his youngest sister protested this arrangement, and even smirked that "the self-proclaimed king in this house has no slaves." Finally, he may conclude that he is in that sister's debt. For, without her hectoring, he might be divorced several times by now.

So too, the following reviewers started with the tunes, picked out the metaphors and allowed the unintended metaphorical allusions to guide the free associations that ensued.

Spence

When Spence began to sing the lyrics of *But Not For Me,* almost the entire group joined in. He explained that his parents had so enjoyed George and Ira Gershwin's *Crazy for You,*[2] that throughout his youth his mother hummed and sang this lead tune. He chose these lines for a metaphor:

> *I know that love's a game;*
> *I'm puzzled just the same,*
> *Was I the moth or the flame?*
> *I'm all at sea.*

Long ago Spence had decided he was "the flame," and "not only because the girls were crazy about me." He had become a teacher "to enlighten young minds," and then a guidance counselor "to help the kids still in the dark." When the facilitator asked Spence to continue his associations with the metaphor, he answered:

"Flame" reminds me of the beeswax candles made in Syracuse, New York, where I grew up. It was a city of ethnic neighborhoods, and the only exception to the homogeneity on our block was the flamboyant widow who lived directly across from us. She kept Santa's sleigh and reindeer illuminated on her lawn throughout the year, and spent the entire summer hosing herself on the front stoop. Each spring she painted the lowest five feet of the maple tree at her curb a different color. To my mother's chagrin, on the morning of my sister's wedding, she was covering it fire engine red.

Last year I was in Syracuse for a conference, and decided to visit my old homestead. When I rang my doorbell to ask permission to walk around the property, a woman and a teenage grandson answered. After I explained that I grew up in her house, she asked me several questions about my mother. When my replies matched what her neighbors had told her, she was satisfied that I was telling the truth. Then to my surprise, she continued, "I'm Mrs. Rosen. We bought the house from the people you sold it to. Unfortunately we have had a great deal of sorrow here. Would you like to go through the house, and tell me some amusing memories about each of the rooms? It might help me enjoy the house more." Her grandson nodded vigorously at the suggestion.

Of course, all three of us enjoyed the memories that flooded me. I told them about locking the housekeeper in the living room coat closet for two hours when I was five. In the adjoining dining room, I recalled how I replaced the forty-watt bulbs in the chandelier with ones of higher wattage to brighten my parents' silver anniversary party. During the dinner, though, the extra heat snapped off a glass pendant which stabbed the roast beef on the maid-of-honor's plate.

On the second floor outside my bedroom, I silently remembered running out to find my mother standing on this very spot, pounding the wall and sobbing because she had just discovered that my father had died during the night. While I was lost in this reverie, Mrs. Rosen touched my arm and beamed, "Your merry stories will help me to enjoy this house too!" But I was cornered within my own memories, and hoping to recover my equilibrium, I told her that I needed to leave now to be on time for my plane.

At the front door Mrs. Rosen said that from now on she would regard this house "as our common home." As I thanked her again for her hospitality, I asked whether the widow still lived across the street. "Ah, yes," she smiled. "Soon after we arrived, some neighborhood kids on their bicycles shouted anti-Semitic names at our house. When they rode by a second time, she soaked them with her hose, and crossed the street to tell me, 'Welcome! I'm glad you moved here!'"

This has been powerful. What started with a "flame" became a blaze of memories. Some hurt me, some comforted me, and they're all enriched me.

Paradoxical metaphor led Spence to become a guest in his own home, to discover that his private distress liberated Mrs. Rosen, and recast the widowed neighbor, his family's bête noir, as a heroine.

Sidney

Sidney blurted out that Spence and he must be relatives. He too grew up in a family that gathered around the piano each night to sing show tunes, including many by George and Ira Gershwin. A favorite of his was *Lorelei or Pardon My English* from the show *My Cousin in Milwaukee*.[3] His rendition included the lines:

> *Her singing isn't operatic;*
> *It's got a lot of static,*
> *But makes your heart get acrobatic*
> *Nine times out of ten.*

> *O, my heart's "acrobatic," all right, only it didn't require any singing. I was born before penicillin, and rheumatic fever almost did me in. I lived on digitalis for ages. But right now, acrobatic is conjuring up the image of doing a routine on the high wire without a safety net. 'Cause that's me; no safety net. I've always been self-employed and relied on my own wits. In the beginning I was pretty successful, but I invested in stocks that should have done better, and sold them before they finally did do better. I have to thank my wife's family that I eventually recovered my equilibrium. Ordinarily I wouldn't have listened to them, but they were really kind, not critical or preachy. But it was hard to accept help from in-laws! I've gotten even, though, by being able to help a couple of their kids who didn't want to "hear anything" from their own parents.*

The associations Sidney made with "acrobatic" led him from seeing himself as handicapped and financially imprudent to appreciating his generative role as a "Dutch uncle" to the following generation.

Lucia

Lucia is an eighty-two year old great-grandmother. About ten years ago, her daughter celebrated Lucia's birthday by taking her to *Gypsy*.[4] Lucia bought her own album of the show soon after, and even now could sing the lyrics from her favorite song, *Together Wherever We Go*:

> *All out or all in,*
> *And whether it's win, place, or show,*
> *With you for me and me for you,*
> *We'll muddle through whatever we do.*

> *Isn't the rhythm of the song catchy? It reminds me of our family's excitement and courage when we left Italy. We had paisans here but no relatives. But in a couple of years my father had his own grocery store with my brothers helping him and speaking English. They also screened every fellow who wanted to*

meet me. In order to go to a movie on the first date with my future husband, the entire family had to come, with the two of us sitting at each end! But it all worked out, like the song says.

We stuck together no matter what, but I never appreciated how much of a gamble we took. That "what" happened a lot by chance. I can see where I've taken credit for what were really "lucky breaks," and I've tended to judge others when they haven't been so lucky. When my son-in-law's mother got lung cancer, I figured that she was a big smoker. But I learned she didn't smoke at all. Then my cousin got fired from his job as a hospital elevator operator for sassing a doctor. I wasn't surprised 'cause he never could mind his own business. But I learned the story—that he overheard a surgeon telling another doctor on the elevator that a patient my cousin knew was "a real bitch." As the doctors exited, my cousin told the surgeon, "And you're a stupid bastard who ought to watch his own mouth!" I am so proud of him! This is a great lesson for me. Hopefully I can start cutting people some slack when I hear about them or remember them. Well, maybe not the surgeon.

The paradoxical metaphor led Lucia along a circuitous route that included humility, appreciating the courage of others confronting their own challenges, and the resolve to be more tolerant.

Rabija

Rabija is eighty years old, born and married in Kashmir. She and her husband emigrated to the United States in 1953, and had their son Munib three years later. She described Paul Simon and Art Garfunkle's *Bridge Over Troubled Water* as a song she cherished.[5] It embodied the couple's commitment to helping others escape the warring, "troubled water" between Pakistanis and Indians in their homeland. Her husband worked in a refrigerated warehouse, and she worked as clerk and cashier in a delicatessen. For twenty years they used their incomes to pay for their relatives' emigration, to provide hospitality, and then guide them in finding employment.

When the facilitator asked what else Rabija associated with "bridge," she answered:

You know, towers on suspension bridges offer ideal nesting sites for hawks. You can have people and raptors in the same location, doing their own thing and oblivious to each other. Something like that happened with the "bridge work" of our family.

We finally had to stop our "bridging" when Munib started an affair with the daughter of distant relatives who were staying with us. The affair caused tremendous contention in the household, and when all the parents agreed that the two should marry, our son ran away. We have had no contact with him since, though we have been contributing to his daughter's support. I haven't brought this up before because I've felt so ashamed. A neighbor said we neglected Munib. Even though we included him in rescuing our families, I guess we couldn't be the bridge's roadway and tower at the same time. Yet, his silence all these months, his neglecting his child—our family is not like that. He is more like the hawk, using the bridge but not part of it.

Her colleagues vied to speak. One urged Rubija to consider how American culture had influenced Munib. Another wondered whether Munib's "windswept flight from his nest" might yet benefit all the parties. "Give it time."

Rabija responded:

We "flew" Kashmir, and yet we never really left. We failed to help Munib try his own wings here, however high they might take him. And now, while an empty nest is always ready for him, it is no less important that we fly more ourselves.

The paradoxical metaphor of "bridging" led Rabija to acknowledge both the value of the services her family performed and also the neglect of Munib that this involved. Finally, it drew her to recognize that a viable future for her husband and her required them to appreciate and address their own needs as a couple.

HOMONYMS

Homonyms are two or more words spelled and pronounced alike but differing in meaning, e.g., *mine, lie.* Homophones are words that sound alike but differ in spelling and meaning, e.g., *rite, write, right, wright.* (Hereafter, "homonym" will refer to either term.)

Facilitators explain that speakers intend only one meaning of a homonym they use to relate an unsettling theme or episode they recall. Then as they did with metaphors, they ask for examples of homonyms from the members. One recalled William Blake's homonym that appears at the head of the chapter, "to *bear* the beams of love." On the one hand, "bear" refers to the capacity to tolerate the brightness of love's radiance. On the other hand, "bear" refers to the capacity to endure the sufferings loving requires. The ambiguity provoked a thoughtful exchange of opinions.

Next, facilitators ask members to identify homonyms when they hear them in one another's speech. Any initial awkwardness passes once they notice how ubiquitously homonyms occur in their conversations. To further ease this interaction, facilitators distribute books listing homonyms for members to consult during the week.[6]

The participants usually respond spiritedly to the lists, clarifying the different meanings of the terms and again offering homonyms of their own. Finally, they follow the steps used to transpose homonyms into paradoxes. First, they select a homonym from any source, and relate one of its meanings to a particular reminiscence. (In the following examples this intended meaning is capitalized.)

Second, they apply the meaning of the *unintended* sound-mate to the same reminiscence, and pursue the free association which then occurs. Their experience with metaphors has already primed them to trust that free association will fashion a compassionate lens for reviewing their past. Just as it did in converting metaphors to paradoxes, using the unintended term again disrupts the self-assessments and moods originally arising from the reminiscence. The process succeeds, of course, because the members determine the direction their homonyms pursue. "This is my homonym. Ultimately I determine where all its meanings will lead me. Now let's see what more it reveals about my reminiscence!"

Gregory

Gregory is a seventy-five year old retired newspaper editor, who is now a literacy volunteer at his local library. Once a week he stayed after these meetings to participate in a life review group. His own review focused upon the career to which he had committed all his reserves of time and energy. He attributed his two divorces, alienation from his children, and his alcohol abuse to his determination to earn his colleagues' respect as a leader in his field. He chose "BEER/bier" as a homonym pertinent to this theme. He referred to his "beer belly" and "six course liquid lunches," lamenting that now "I am crying in my beer."

When the facilitator asked him to view the theme of constantly needing to prove himself through the lens of "bier" this time, he paused. "Bier" elicited a different sequence of memories. He began haltingly,

> *My parents argued a lot, and I never saw them kiss. Then, at my father's funeral my mother approached the open coffin for the last time, pushed back a curl of my father's hair, and kissed his forehead. The lesson I drew, and have kept to myself, wasn't that she had finally kissed him, but that she had kissed him too late. I wasn't married at the time, and I worried that an intimate relationship could be too late for me as well. I was frightened because I didn't have role models for a gratifying family life. I'm recognizing only now that the compulsiveness I brought to my career felt more manageable than my anxiety about emotional closeness.*

Another participant intervened with the homonym "HEIR/err." She pointed out that Gregory had been "heir" to his family's disordered relationships, and this inheritance had led him to "err," in turn, in the family he began. Other members gave their own examples of equivalent ways in which they too had adapted to subsequent relationships the unfortunate patterns they had adopted from their family of origin. Gregory responded to their shared "erring" by acknowledging that divorces and cutoffs appeared repeatedly throughout his family tree, and that he was perpetuating this pattern now for another generation.

Broken hearted about his children's withdrawal from him, Gregory captured their estrangement in an anecdote about his daughter's graduation.

> *At the dinner party following commencement, I publicly rebuked her for smoking marijuana at the table. She stood at her place, and gave me a Nazi salute. "FUHRER/furor" is the homonym that epitomizes the moment for me. I took her criticism so personally, but such "furor" has characterized our family for generations. I want to spare my grandchildren from our family's rages. I want to bring this larger perspective up with my children, and in the process begin to reconcile with them.*

Paradoxical homonyms led Gregory to recognize how his compulsive careerism had distracted him from his fear of intimacy. The homonyms guided him to reach out to the younger generations, particularly in terms of his passing on the family's "furor."

Agatha

Agatha is a seventy-four year old lawyer forced to retire because of emphysema. Her life review focused upon the compulsivity with which she approached her career and her painfully meticulous preparations for courtroom presentations. Her colleagues pointed out her use of "read" as a homonym term she had used repeatedly. She answered that "REED/read" did resonate with her. She recited a text she had heard so often in church, Isaiah 42:3, "A bruised reed He [sic] will not break; and a smoking flax He will not quench." She then added,

> *But that's the trouble. I bruised myself continuously—obsessing over details, concealing the belief that I was less competent than my colleagues, driven and unable to relax—and all that time succeeded as a lawyer. I could always manage to suffer and read. My forced retirement has left many feelings of emptiness, and I hope that you can appreciate me even as a "bruised reed" that does not have to justify its existence. I can see now that preparing legal briefs had long been my way of keeping doubts about myself at bay, and at last I am allowing myself to feel them.*

The reference to Isaiah prompted another member to raise the homonym "SOUL/sole." He pointed out knowingly:

> *Agatha, you look to the relationships in the group to feel secure in the depths of your "soul." These relationships are certainly here for you, and you know by now that you're not the "sole" super-striver in the group.*

Agatha replied by extending the homonym with a metaphor.

> *"Sole" reminds me of "fillet," and forgive me for the pun, but "I have a bone to pick" with myself for not accepting myself. I absent myself when I deny the way my insecurities have driven me, when I deny the traits I have. The self my friends love is the self I've wanted to change, and now I finally want to embrace. I've been so dense!*

Her comment evoked another participant's homonym, *"We're all 'DENSE/ dents' when it comes to looking at ourselves."* Agatha sat straight up with the insight that acceptance of mutual weaknesses had always been the strongest bond in her friendships. She summarized how her liabilities, not her assets, had been the source of gratifying relationships. *"It's not being exceptional or famous that counts. Our delight is truly in our 'dents'!"*

Fergus

Fergus, a retired physical therapist sitting to Agatha's left, followed with reminiscences that included this excerpt:

> *My sisters taunted me that no one could brighten our mother's day as I could. They remember well how she bragged to the neighbors about my early promotion from kindergarten. You see, she was divorced, and I was her only "SON/sun." So, after getting skipped a grade on two occasions, with much fanfare from my mother, I was really taken back by her answer to my question as an eleven year old, "What makes our nationality any better than others?" She told me simply, "We fight with our hands."*

Fergus took this more as a literal statement of values than a statement of ethnocentric prejudice. He noted that this exchange had occurred at the time when several of his classmates, already in puberty, had begun to lift weights at home and at gyms. He joined them, a runt by comparison, and valued their respect for his scrappiness. In his imagination he would be the next Gene Tunney, a scholarly pugilist.

His mother's reaction to his workouts at the gym surprised him. First, she complained that he did not look up to the task, and would surely get injured. Then, she argued that his workouts were detracting from the time he needed to maintain his test scores. In fact, she did not consider his eventual career choice as a physical therapist up to his talents. The two of them were chronically disappointed with each other for decades.

Fergus's emphasis upon the "SON/sun" homonym showed that he recognized the shaming voice still governing his self-assessment as his mother's and not his own. By hearing this voice as something external to himself, he was beginning the journey toward making it something he could more easily reject as "not me."

Gladys

Seventy-seven year old Gladys brought her own twist to using homonyms. Hemiplegic since her stroke seven years before, she was not able to speak clearly. So she had made copies of these lines from Christopher Fry's *The Lady's Not for Burning*,[7] and, aglow with good humor (LIGHT/light), distributed them to the group:

> *I travel light; as light*
> *That is, as a man can travel who is*
> *Still carrying his body around because*
> *Of its sentimental value.*

Then she distributed this postscript (ASSENT/ascent):

> *Silence means "assent," and I hope that my halted voice somehow expresses acceptance of my condition. You are looking at a woman who is graced in her infirmities. Over the past seven years I have had many lows emotionally, but now I am in "ascent." The very limits the stroke imposed are vantage points that give the grandest perspective on my life. I so agree with this image from Edmund Waller's Old Age:*[8]

> > *The soul's dark cottage, battered and decayed,*
> > *Lets in new light through chinks that*
> > *Time hath made.*

Gladys's efforts in preparing the materials and her evident wisdom moved the group. In keeping with her theme, a colleague smiled, "I'll never make *light* of you, Gladys; it already surrounds you."

Constance and Nell

Constance, aged seventy-nine, and Nell, aged seventy-six, are sisters who live in separate apartments at a life care community. Their relationship involved vigorous arguing with each other or exchanging sarcastic swipes with brief interludes of peace. Whatever the disagreement, the topic invariably included their life-long grievances. Constance complained how she and her late husband had had to rescue Nell repeatedly from "the sordid relationships and financial ruin" that accompanied her sister's alcoholism.

In her life review, Nell began excoriating Constance for her self-righteousness and controlling intrusiveness. She stopped her criticism, however, after getting "a new take" on their relationship from reading the score from *Show Boat* during the week:[9]

> *We've kept at each other all this time because that's how we show we care. It hit me when I was singing "Make Believe" and realized that the song requires that the singer must already be in love in order to pretend to be. So, today, Constance, let's be nice, and act as though we do love each other. In fact, I'll start first and you can tell me each time I've made it through another hour.*

Archie added his own opinion. He is a retired landscaper who now keeps a critical eye on the residence's grounds keepers. "I'm not worried about you two working out your differences. Your family tree is a hickory, ancient and presiding in the garden. It has an anchoring TAP ROOT that conducts all the nutrients for mutual caring that you need." Constance, though, quickly interrupted, "The only *tap route* Nell knows is on a map to a pub." With gentle humor this time, Nell broke the tension by adapting the line from Oscar Wilde, "Constance, you lack only a few vices to be perfect!"

Thus, during this meeting the sisters used both lyrics and homonyms as paradoxes. Though the sisters did not resolve the issues between them, the introduction of humorous, clever observations may be an easing step toward an eventual live-and-let-live acceptance of each other.

Note how homonyms drew out more homonyms. Their use encouraged easy give-and-take, and members regularly profited from examples others raised as much as from their own. They were helping one another "to bear the beams of love" more gently and more lightly.

Chapter Ten

Intergenerational Paradox

For any activity framed in a particular way one is likely to find another activity that is systematically disattended and treated as out of frame, something not to be given any concern or attention . . . [though] more consequential, perhaps, for the main activity than the first.—Frame Analysis[1]

Sooner or later older adults reviewing their life give their "concern or attention" to two family "frames." The first frame includes the dynamics which enmeshed them in toxic issues and triangles, primarily the quality of their relationship with their parents. The second frame includes the dynamics through which they, in turn, enmeshed their children in these issues and triangles. With themselves as the pivoting generation in these frames, however, older adults are frequently left with a grievance against their parents and guilt toward their children.

In the text at the head of this chapter, Erving Goffman points out that a perspective focusing on certain details in a frame may distract attention from more explanatory details evident from a different perspective. With this in mind, facilitators encourage reviewers to shift from the perspective of being the pivotal generation to the "disattended" perspective of their families transmitting scripts over five generations. This intergenerational overview catches compelling and extenuating circumstances that reframe grievances and guilt through more compassionate lenses. It is the paradox of managing memories by attending to the flowing transmission of scripted behavior over generations rather than by focusing primarily on the reviewers' role in the transmission.

AN AERIAL OVERVIEW OF FIVE GENERATIONS

This longitudinal perspective begins by acknowledging issues currently roiling relationships between the family's two youngest generations, i.e., between the reviewers' children and grandchildren. At this distance, reviewers can be more observers than participants, and notice how their children, without plan or malice, continue to pass on toxic issues to their own children. They witness how family scripts remain in place even as the actors change.

Then, as members of life review groups move up a generation, they bring this insight to these same issues playing out between themselves and their children. Of course, these reminiscences often evoke the conflicting emotions accompanying their assessment of themselves as parents. Accordingly, facilitators urge reviewers to proceed another generation back, recalling how comparable issues occurred in their relationship with their own parents. Again, the emotions accompanying unresolved issues from their childhood and adolescence often elicit judgments blaming their parents' behavior. The reviewers may still have difficulty empathizing with their parents and appreciating the clutch that recurring issues had upon all the parties involved.

Thus, reviewers need to proceed back one generation further, and reflect upon memories and anecdotes about interactions between their father and his parents and their mother and her parents. Family folklore that reveals the transmission of scripts to and from ancestors is especially enlightening at this point.

There are two benefits from these repeated shifts of focus over the generations. First, the shifting shows that self-acceptance means embracing a self in large part prescribed by the family's scripting. Second, reviewers' memories about the programmed transmission of toxic issues from their grandparents' generation to their own both minimize self-preoccupation while encouraging acceptance of their own role in compounding the lives of their grandchildren.

This attention to the family transmission of scripts tempers the severity with which reviewers evaluate themselves and others. They can see how they and their contemporaries behaved in the very fashion that they had criticized in previous generations. Indeed, their children and grandchildren may find them wanting by the same standards that the reviewers applied to their forebears. The uninterrupted flow of family dysfunction does not excuse the reviewers' own input. At some point they became the adults responsible for the wellbeing of the generation in their care. The extenuating circumstances surrounding the flow do not excuse irresponsible behavior. These circumstances can, however, arouse compassion among generations for one another.

Finally, this aerial overview can draw older adults beyond their reminiscences to greater concern with the wellbeing of younger generations. As they recognize the replication of toxic issues, triangles, slogans, and epitaphs among their grandchildren, they can gently try to modify their own patterns of interacting with younger kin. Dispassionately, even humorously, they can also point to their own life as an object lesson concerning the influence that scripts can have.

SCRIPTED SELF AS PARADOX

Facilitators encourage reviewers to recast the intergenerational content in the form of three paradoxes. The first paradox is the ability to appreciate that personal autonomy involves members owning the family script passed on to them.

Eileen

Eileen is an eighty-three year old widow whose son and daughter-in-law asked her to move into their home. Her cardiac condition was deteriorating, and they had room available now that fourteen year old Philip was the only child living at home. Eileen was ambivalent about the move because she knew that her son and Philip regularly quarreled. Her poor health and her warm relationship with her daughter-in-law finally induced her to accept.

About two weeks after Eileen had moved in, an argument broke out during dinner. Philip had responded in a sassy tone of voice to his mother's request that he mow the lawn the following day after school. Philip's father pounded the table, shouting his outrage about his son's audacity. Philip rushed outdoors and the others finished eating in silence. After everyone but the father had left the table, Philip returned with a large scrape on his elbow from falling off his bicycle. He said nothing about the scrape, and approached his father, crying, "I can't take being ordered around anymore." The father remained relatively calm and persuaded his son to let him dress the elbow.

After the father and son finished talking, the father directed Philip to apologize to Eileen for the scene at dinner. When he came to her room, Eileen thanked Philip for his courtesy, and then located the upset within the patterns of their family. Philip listened attentively as she spoke about her own father:

His temper was a smoldering fuse, and we tried not to provoke him. Hardness would enter his voice as he gripped one hand with the other. When he had this demeanor, we asked no questions, dropped what we were about, and did whatever he wanted. When I married your grandfather against my father's wishes, he refused to attend the wedding. When the rest of my family came, he really hardened his heart. Only my children were able to bring him and me together—five years after the wedding.

I was like a volcano myself. Outside the family people loved me for being humorous and doing favors. I enjoyed my family too, but I'd get bothered when the children didn't do things the way I wanted and when I wanted them done. I knew about my temper, so I'd warn them by whistling for a while. If they didn't shape up then, I'd give it to them. I remember kicking your father twice. When he was twelve I gave it to him in front of the house because he hadn't practiced the violin that day. Then, when he was your age, I kicked over the kitchen chair he was on. He had been fooling around so much that he missed the bus for school.

Your father hardly ever acted up when he was a teenager. It worried me a little because I knew that he had to be burying his anger inside. Sometimes it would slip out. At his sister's graduation from college, he wanted my attention while I was talking to a friend. When I didn't stop right away, he dug his fingernails into my wrist. Another time, when he was sixteen, he pulled a practical joke that upset me terribly. His father and I came home from a movie to find him stretched out on the kitchen floor with a wound in his head. As soon as I gasped, he jumped up and shouted, "Fooled you!" His wound was only catsup. He apologized after we told him how upsetting his ruse had been. He said he had gotten the idea from a comic book he was reading.

I think he's better off now, fussing as he does with you instead of keeping it in. It's no picnic for you, I know, but you're doing better than he did at your age. I think you have the savvy to handle your responsibilities and to learn from your father.

That was a graced moment for Philip and Eileen. She used her life review to explain anger as a master theme in both their lives, to describe its permutations through the generations, and to raise the boy's empathy for his father. She used her own experience to illustrate the inevitability of excess and mistakes in coping with anger. Not least for Eileen, she avoided the snare of interjecting herself between father and son.

Frances

Frances is a seventy year old retired architect who described herself as a workaholic without a job, an extrovert without friends, and a mother with uneasy contacts with her children. She decided to identify the slogan and epitaph she thought colleagues and children would concur best describe her and then to do the same with kin in different generations.

For herself she applied the slogan, *Prime the pump.* She had pursued professional education that prepared her for a career in architecture. A novice in the predominantly male occupation at the time, she demonstrated her competence by routinely doing the work of two colleagues while collaborating with an interdisciplinary team of engineers, contractors, lawyers, and public officials.

For herself she chose the epitaph, *She's the power behind the throne.* Frances married a pilot who was frequently away from the family. When she was managing a single parent household, she "ran a tight ship" scheduling meals and after school activities for her two sons. Later, when Frances was first widowed, she moved to a residence hotel, and used this time to select a life care community.

Frances then spoke about her mother Elise who attended teachers' training school, and taught in the Baltimore school system for thirty-one years. She married the manager of a prominent department store, and over the years referred her most reliable students to him for employment. Elise was proudest of two episodes involving her career. One was her public support for hiring as teachers members of the Abraham Lincoln Brigade. They had fought as American volunteers on the side of the Republic during the Spanish Civil War. When they returned, many were harassed as communists, and encountered significant resistance when they sought teaching positions.

The second episode concerned Elise's intransigence in the face of Frances's relentless efforts to make her retire. Frances had a sister five years older than herself who would escort her to and from school and stay with her until Elise got home. Frances, however, would have none of this arrangement. Over a six month period while she was in first grade, Frances feigned stomach upsets, threw chalk and scissors at her sister, and hyperventilated in the classroom. Elise did not relent, however, and after all kinds of fits and starts, Frances acquiesced.

Frances thought that the slogan, *Bell the cat,* captured Elise's script. Frances preferred this slogan because she lifted it from the *Piers Ploughman* text Elise taught, in which the mice decide to put a bell around the cat's neck as a warning device, but then can find none among them to do the job. Elise would do the job!

Frances also used as an epitaph for Elise, *She brought others to heel.* On the one hand, she could appreciate her mother's discipline with students and her advocacy with the board of education. On the other hand, Frances repeated that she felt forced "like an animal" to obey her mother's insistence that she attend school.

Finally, Frances spoke about her maternal grandmother Aude who emigrated from La Rochelle, France, as a seventeen-year old indentured servant to escape an arranged marriage. She worked through her contract over the next decade, apprenticed to a dressmaker, and then opened her own establishment. She sang in the choir of the Huguenot church, and several of its communicants courted her. She married a postman, and then worked out of their home. She was also widely credited for her husband becoming a postal service inspector. Aude had three miscarriages before giving birth to Elise, her only living child and Frances's mother.

Frances remembered her mother had a slogan that captured Aude's attitudes and behavior, *Make your bricks even without straw.* Frances appreciated it because it emphasized that her grandmother was able to accomplish her tasks even without the necessary means to do so.

Frances's epitaph for Aude was, "*She made the grade.*" Frances enjoyed this epitaph because she could pun that Aude not only succeeded in satisfying rigorous requirements, but also did this going up hill all the way.

A few sessions later Frances drew upon her awareness of the intergenerational descent of slogans and epitaphs. She saw, first of all, that she bore a legacy of "making the better the enemy of the good." She needed to ease into satisfactory, "good enough" relationships with others.

Frances was adept at commanding attention, though it had often reduced relationships with her children's families to ritual, rather than caring, encounters. Now she began limiting calls to her daughters-in-law to one a week, and inquiring about the activities of her grandchildren instead of giving advice. In response, they invited her to their family activities more often, and Frances relaxed into proud and enjoyable attendance at her grandchildren's dance and orchestral recitals, dramas, and athletic events. Finally, she chose to extend her contacts beyond the family and volunteered her services as an art instructor in an after school program that provided transportation for her.

THE DIP-TO-RISE PARADOX

The second paradox requires reviewers to accept family life as a series of ascending spirals that "dip-to-rise" with a gaping differential between the discomfort of the dip and the comparatively slight rise that it precedes. The dips consist of family members' anxiety arising from testing out assumptions, problem solving strategies, and different points of view. The rises consist of higher levels of performance, interactional skills, and self-esteem that result when reviewers bear the anxiety and pleasantly discover that it was an inadequate measure of their capabilities.

The spiraling, of course, is continuous. As generations proceed through the life cycle, the solutions to earlier problems become new problems, knowledge becomes obsolete, crises become opportunities, latent talents become more gratifying than individuals' "strong suit," and, hopefully, models of hierarchical authority yield to inclusive decision making. Each level of higher functioning becomes a bench mark from which to dip and rise to an ever more gratifying level of fulfillment. Throughout the spiraling, however, the dips exact an emotional toll exquisitely more pronounced than the satisfaction of the rise.

Lois

Lois is an eighty-two year old widow who had recently been diagnosed with terminal cancer, and has found gratifying support from the members of life review group. Her brother's family had invited her to an engagement party for their granddaughter, but her health prevented her from attending. One of her hobbies, however, included photography, and she offered to videotape her account about family history. At a recent session of her life review group Lois showed the video.

Lois wanted to convey the emphasis that her family placed on matters of health because this topic had been ruinously toxic for her. She was the youngest of three siblings, a brother followed by two sisters. Her brother attended their father's high school where he excelled as a running back on the football team. Their father had been a varsity defensive tackle on the same team. As adults, Lois's brother was an accomplished yachtsman, and her sister, captain of her high school's field hockey team, taught physical education classes for thirty years.

Lois, however, was born with extremely poor eyesight that five surgeries had only marginally improved. Her parents were overprotective about her engaging in any outdoor activities, and her siblings nicknamed her "Cy" for Cyclops. She felt deeply about being left out of the family's athletic pastimes.

On the other hand, Lois was musically gifted with perfect pitch that she brought to the piano and the harp. She attended college on a music scholarship, and met her husband when they played together in the college orchestra. He later played in the pit for Broadway musicals while she gave lessons at home. She postponed practicing for recitals while raising their children, and found her most satisfying professional outlet as pianist for the local community theater.

Because she was physically compromised, the family folklore and traditions held no place for her. They touted vigor, physical risk, and longevity, beginning with Lois's great-grandfather, the town's longest living veteran of the Grand Army of the Republic. Her older relatives regularly blamed any kin who died "prematurely" in their seventies for "bringing it on through their own fault." Similarly, her grandmother, an Irish immigrant, used to intone the humorous, but telling, point that "back home we had to shoot a man to start a cemetery!"

Lois's mother had suffered severely from life long asthma, but denying the risks involved, insisted on enrolling in physical education courses. When she did die in middle age, the extended family enthused about "how vigorous" she looked in the coffin. Once Lois's father turned sixty, he developed high blood pressure, and would wake up at night with blood flowing from his nose. He simply wiped it off, and returned to sleep. Though he was laden with arthritis that had him going up and down stairs on his backside, he still traveled by trolley to work daily.

Lois told her group that her granddaughter had thanked her for the videotape and assured her, "Let me tell you, I have no intention of carrying on this health-madness!" Then, Lois spoke of the "rises" she now could see had occurred astride her "dips":

> *Juilliard admitted three of my harp students, and one of my piano students is touring now in China as accompanist for an opera diva. And I feel freer now that I see that there was "nothing personal" in the dismissive attitudes I received at home. A picture comes to me of my parents and siblings standing under a long running shower of "health blinders." But that's not how it was. They were really struggling for their footing under a waterfall! In their flailing, they knocked me down, but at last I'm no longer knocking myself down too. And I've stopped feeling abandoned by kin for not visiting me more when, truth be known, they can't bear to acknowledge the reality that someday they will be dying like me. Well, to use my family's idiom, I'm about "to cross the finish line" in peace.*

Lois's life review is her way of claiming meaning for her life now that she is dying. It expresses her absolution of others who have harassed or dismissed her. It is her gift to her colleagues for their support of her. It enables us to understand the intergenerational transmission that forecast the parameters influencing her life

MEND CUTOFFS

In addition to opining about who is correctly managing a current crisis or giving advice about the best ways to proceed, family members can also discuss previous incarnations over the generations of the issues now at hand. In this way, the past can provide kin with the perspective that issues are currently driving them as they did their predecessors. Assessing blame is a distraction while a contagious anxiety is consuming mutual respect.

Simone

Simone is a seventy-three year old divorcee who had managed an inn with her ex-husband in a picturesque California town. She had sold the business, and spent the next two years at her family homestead near Lyon. Her life review included her role in reconciling family members embroiled in the intergenerational dispute that ensued.

During her years in France, a "great break" occurred in her family. When a cousin announced that she was marrying a Nigerian, her own generation in the family boycotted the wedding en masse. The exception was another cousin who sent a searing letter to her relatives condemning their intolerance. When Simone returned, she kept up amicable ties with her entire family, even though the alienated parties avoided contact with each other.

> *I reached out to the adult children of the embattled parties to help me organize a reception at which I would show the videos of my years abroad. At this planning meeting, I spoke candidly of the family rift. I noted how those present had nothing to do with it, yet they were being deprived of one another's camaraderie. I asked, as a gift to me, that they urge their parents to attend the reception.*
>
> *When the event began, I greeted all my relatives by name, and had them choose their own tables. Then, I thanked my helping kin for their generous teamwork. I shared humorous memories about members my generation in attendance. Finally, I asked them to share reminiscences of me, since this could be one of the few remaining opportunities I might have to hear their stories. I closed by speaking of my regret that I was inaccessible during "our great break," and could not help them repair its consequences.*
>
> *The first relative I called to speak was the cousin who wrote the inflammatory letter. Before she even began reminiscing, this cousin first apologized for the letter's self-righteous tone. After she finished, I asked for another speaker, and one of the boycott leaders volunteered. He said how he had had many second thoughts over the rift but, like others, had not reopened the matter during family social occasions. After several other reparatory—and humorous—speakers, the new groom broke up the party by announcing, "I only wanted to marry in because I heard you all had lots of money!"*

The weight of family distress that Simone bore, the intolerance, guilt, and stubbornness, reappeared in the reflections of each speaker. This time, however, as kin were dipping-to-rise with gratitude for the chance to air it all, the larger family could better share the weight.

Beatrice

A second example of mending cutoffs concerns Beatrice, a seventy-nine year old widow. At a recent funeral she learned that her granddaughter and her husband were considering separating as the first step toward a divorce.

Beatrice called them, and they agreed to visit her. She wanted to encourage them to keep self-disclosing, open communications with each other, since she regretted the way she had accommodated her husband's audacious unilateral decision making.

He insisted, for instance, when they were hosting guests, that she prepare him an entrée different from the one she was serving everyone else. While he was dying, he demanded that she support him to the car so that he could eat at his favorite clam bar. She acquiesced, drove through the snow, and had a waiter serve him at the car. Now, after a lifetime of deferring to others, even moderate assertiveness on her part felt too pushy to her.

Beatrice pointed out to the couple that both her grandmother and mother had soured their marriages by making unilateral decisions that their husbands had to confront after the fact. Her grandmother, for instance, arranged for her three brothers to board with her for six months after they immigrated together to America. When her husband, a warehouse manager, discovered them at his home, he moved into the warehouse for the duration of their stay. When the brothers finally asked her why she did not discuss her plans with her husband beforehand, she replied, "What, and have two fights!"

On the other hand, her grandfather did not make it easy for his wife to consult with him. Beatrice remembered that her grandfather had emigrated from Ukraine in 1890, even though he would have inherited the farm. He "wanted more" for himself, and arrived in New York City already speaking some English. She recalled the folklore that he spent so much time in the attic studying that family members "had to schedule appointments to see him." As he grew older, decrements from a long standing pulmonary condition isolated him even further from socializing with his extended family.

In the ensuing generation Beatrice's mother continued the practice of making unilateral decisions. When Beatrice's grades remained just above failing after two years of high school, her mother sent her, without consulting her husband, to a boarding school in a neighboring state. Then, when she was graduating, her mother picked out a finishing school for her and even the courses she would take there.

Beatrice reminisced that her father distanced himself much like her grandfather. He was a basement tinkerer who had acquired several patents, and was inaccessible to the family for days and nights at a time. When her mother turned to Beatrice for a compensatory relationship, she felt "suffocated," and distanced into her secretarial employment. Her mother then became enmeshed with her sister, instead. When her granddaughter's husband inquired how the family atmosphere affected its members, Beatrice noted that her siblings had moved out of state once they were adults "just for the breathing room."

Beatrice added that until she shared this history, she had not appreciated how significantly her grandmother's and mother's assertiveness and her own mousiness were two sides of the same coin. She had urged the couple to recognize the reciprocal two-step that the generations of married couples played out. Yes, one party may lead the dance and contribute more dramatically to their shared dysfunction, but the other party contributes in turn. Who is more flagrant is irrelevant in terms of ending the dance. Each party has to recognize, she concluded, how he or she "is making the mess worse."

As Beatrice reminisced with the group, she was amazed that she had stirred herself to invite her granddaughter and husband to meet with her. Arranging their get-together showed her that she did have the reserves of self-esteem to be more assertive, even if her stomach was churning with anxiety. Her plan in the months ahead was to write to her cousins-in-law whose company she had enjoyed and with whom she had not kept up contact after her husband's death. Then, she would bring herself to telephone them. She would call upon her newly appreciated assertiveness to work through cutoffs. "I certainly am slow, but I'm getting it now!"

The paradoxes above did, indeed, enable reviewers to appreciate aspects of their life review that had heretofore been "systematically disattended and treated as out of frame." The couple did eventually divorce. They proceeded using a mediator, however, rather than lawyers, and parted fairly amicably with each accepting responsibility.

Chapter Eleven

The Paradox of Metaphysical Self

Vital spark of heav'nly flame!
Quit, o quit this mortal frame;
Trembling, hoping, ling'ring, flying,
O the pain, the bliss of dying!
Cease, fond Nature, cease they strife,
And let me languish into life.
—The Dying Christian to His Soul[1]

These lines, of course, express Alexander Pope's reflections on people's innate ambivalence toward dying. They refer no less to the paradox of metaphysical self which posits that humankind, at its nascent *spark*, resides in an eternal *flame*. The self that all in turn identify as "I," that *fond Nature*, bears the *strife* inherent in the entanglements of epigenetic and family scripted histories. Release, recourse, humankind's shared liberating purpose lies not in its assertions and accomplishments, but in *languishing*, i.e., in acceptance of a gifted dignity already received. When reminiscences obscure, even deny, such dignity, an interchange with facilitators and colleagues can invigorate the *spark*.

Facilitators raise this perspective with group members so that they can foresee how ultimately gratifying the "darkness" in their reminiscences can be. In this paradox reviewers' self-esteem proceeds from the Absolute's esteem for them, and their self-knowledge from an awareness of their self as already compassionately known. From this perspective, reviewers accept themselves because they have already been accepted "by that which is greater than themselves."

Facilitators introduce metaphysical paradox by distributing to their groups excerpted passages of Eastern and Western mystical literature readily available in libraries. Each group member reads any single excerpt in one week, and passes it on to a colleague at the next session. The culturally idiomatic expressions in works from Asian and Islamic spirituality are particularly engaging, and typically elicit an expansive exchange of insight, self-disclosure, and continuing feedback.

A few members want to recover particular passages from a familiar source, others are curious about content of traditions other than their own, and many choose randomly from sources with which they are unfamiliar. Group members with no religious beliefs are often curious about mysticism, and join in comparing its expression in different traditions. The following examples illustrate two themes of metaphysical paradox that buttress older adults' self-esteem.

MYSTICAL NIGHT

When religiously committed reviewers acknowledge that their self-acceptance rests ultimately upon the Absolute's acceptance of them, they may have no tangible experience to confirm this is the case. Whatever initial exhilaration accompanied their awareness of metaphysical self did not release them from dysfunctional personal characteristics. What benefit does metaphysical self offer when reviewers experience it only as so much emptiness, even nothingness?

Shirley

Shirley is an eighty-two year old retired hotel concierge who offered her own life review as answer. First, she commented wryly that metaphysical self seemed unreachable in some "mystical night," and quoted from *The Cloud of Unknowing:*

> *When you first begin, you find only darkness and as it were a cloud of unknowing. . . . Do what you will, this darkness and this cloud remain between you and God, and stop you from seeing him [sic] in the clear light of rational understanding, and from experiencing his loving sweetness in your affection. Reconcile yourself to wait in this darkness as long as is necessary, but still go on longing after him whom you love. For if you are to feel him or to see in this life, it must always be in this cloud, in this darkness. . . . Though your natural mind can now find "nothing" to feed on, for it thinks that you are doing nothing, go on doing this nothing, and do it for the love of God.*[2]

This excerpt moved Shirley to point out how its paradoxical injunctions had her "stay in the dark in order to see, long for the unapproachably clouded Person, and do nothing for the love of God!" By baffling her intellect, though, the passage also enticed Shirley to be alert for more compassionate, inclusive lessons arising from her life review.

She proceeded to show her use of the paradox as she recalled the curiosity and stick-to-itiveness that ensured her competence in the work place.

> *In fact, these two traits became my strong points to such an extent that I had difficulty in withholding unasked for advice and in not usurping others' tasks which I could do more efficiently. But then I began to realize that I had discounted "wonder" as an ingredient of self-fulfillment, and began to notice how my colleagues were making their own contributions. Now I find that our own group is a catalyst for spontaneous memories that catch me unaware. I'm even paying more attention to the activities of other persons in the scenes I remember.*
>
> *In our feedback to one another I'm finding light in my mystical night. Your memories are helping me to see how the overlapping relationships across generations and households are part of me. "Self" is really a plural noun. I can't keep track of the patterns interacting in me. No, let me just accept them, and, however convoluted they are, be grateful for them.*

Shirley found in the mystical night a rationale for suspending judgment about her own life. She could neither access the Absolute nor review her life with photographical precision. She could only approach her memories in attentive passivity, awaiting those gifted intimations which pointed to metaphysical self in her reminiscences.

Norman

Norman is a seventy-four year old retired dentist who asked to be the next to speak. He recalled a scene between his father and himself when he was ten years old. A department store manager had caught him trying to shoplift and contacted his father. In a lecture that evening on the urgency of honesty, his father told him an anecdote from his own youth. When he was in the eighth grade, the Latin teacher had promised a ticket to a World Series baseball game to the student who earned the highest grade on the next examination. The dentist's father and another student tied for the highest grade. In front of the class, the teacher had the boys toss a coin and Norman's father won. When the teacher reviewed the examination with the class, Norman's father discovered an error that the teacher had missed, and told the teacher that the other student should get the ticket. At an honors' convocation later in the week, however, the principal recounted the episode to the entire student body, and awarded tickets to both boys.

Norman's father did not stop there, but traced his family's stress upon honesty still further back. During that lecture, he took from the mantelpiece bronzed shoes that served as bookends, and pointed out their worn heels and soles. He explained that he had bronzed these shoes to memorialize his own grandfather's integrity. Norman's grandfather was an immigrant who settled in Chicago and joined the police force. According to family lore, when he inquired about the procedures for being promoted to sergeant, a captain had replied that a bribe given to him would secure the promotion. Instead, he resigned and *walked* to New York City where he joined the fire department, and was promoted to chief through civil service examinations. These were the shoes he wore on that trek! Norman, of course, recognized that this tale was clearly apocryphal, yet over the generations it had served its purpose. Norman continued,

> *The upshot of all this is I became scrupulously honest in my own relationships. But more, I kept lecturing my sons on this theme, and closely monitored their behavior when they became adolescents. It all backfired. One son, caught up in drugs, stole from us and his employer. Another profited from insider trading in stocks. When I confronted him, he thought he could mollify me simply by agreeing to give half of his ill-gotten gains to charity.*
>
> *I was so upright I could have been a telephone pole! And so blind to how my posturing affected my sons' behavior. Then, for our group meeting today I read, "It is in the very negation of knowledge, in the higher darkness, that the essence of true knowledge is present."[3] I can see how the "honesty" obsession wrapped me in darkness high and low. First, I had to be stumped, and only now can I see the larger picture.*
>
> *I was so earnest about earning acceptance when it was a gift before me all the time. I've been walking a tight rope when I could have been at ease and still been true to myself. Worse, I concealed the joy of metaphysical self from my children by making my approval of them so conditional. No more of this. My boys are adults now, and have family issues of their own. I'm going to be there for them and their families whenever they need me.*

Norman recognized the intergenerational cascade propelling "honesty" as a toxic issue. This helped him to accept his own role in transmitting the issue to his sons. From his darkness in making honesty toxic has come knowledge of the limits of his acceptance of his sons. Now that he understands that they have lived out the counter side of honesty, Norman wants to reach out to them in adult roles that can transcend parent and child.

ENGAGED DETACHMENT

Engaged detachment, a second paradox, expresses another way metaphysical self may appear in life review. This oxymoron refers to reviewers investing themselves whole heartedly in responsibilities, causes, and relationships while accepting that they may never achieve any of their goals. It focuses upon process: the affirmation that we shall die unfinished, our potential only partially realized, and that completion is ultimately beyond us. The Islamic mystical tradition, for instance, expressed this theme, "Give up desire. Think that whatever you get is what you want, and in this acceptance find ease and joy. Renounce desire a hundred times."[4]

Johann

Johann is a seventy-five year old widower and recently retired chief executive of the logging company he founded. He shared with his group how this passage on engaged detachment thoroughly contradicted the dominant theme in his life: winning. Johann was descended from a line of "winners." He had been raised with stories of how his Slovakian immigrant grandfather won promotions from his mail room position through a series of money saving recommendations. He shared his memories of his mother in her fifties, arthritis notwithstanding, besting her siblings in fiercely contested games of handball. He recalled the faded parchments framed on their living room wall testifying to his parents' membership in ARISTA, their high school honors society.

As a child, Johann basked in his mother's preening to neighbors about his grammar school I.Q. scores. He recalled his jealousy when his mother complimented a friend's performance in a high school play in which he also had a part. He remembered his public challenge at his cousin's graduation that he would win ten medals when he graduated for the one awarded her that day. Indeed, he had graduated first in his class from high school, and won a scholarship to college.

Then he began to speak of his only child, a daughter. Johann remembered her tears as an adolescent whenever she lost to him at chess. In senior year of high school she applied only for early acceptance to Stanford and was accepted. Then, after her second year she transferred to Oxford University, and settled permanently in England. His visits to her were the only times they saw each other.

> *So, where did winning get me? Like my forebears, my daughter and I seemed to seek the discipline involved in winning as much as the accomplishment itself. My grandparents' ambition for social mobility set a family trajectory which we've followed fiercely ever since. I don't discount my life as so much loss, but I'm on to the folly of my family's winning ways. I hope to be more*

caring in reaching out to my daughter. She saw me at my worst when my wife was terminally ill. I had to win again. I ordered every kind of experimental treatment, dismissed her request for hospice, and put her through so much pain.

   It's too late for my wife, but perhaps I can reach out to my daughter with fewer expectations of succeeding in our relationship. Hopefully, I can love her without an agenda.

Is it possible to love without expectations about the relationship? Johann saw the hazards of imposing his goals, and was open now to letting the relationship with his daughter evolve.

Roseanna

Seventy-four year old Roseanna is a divorced, recovering alcoholic who achieved sobriety in A.A. twelve years before. Her husband also drank heavily, and when he was drunk, regularly assaulted her. When he was sober, he was irritable and critical of her supposed deficiencies as wife, mother, and housekeeper. Their daughter fled the nastiness between her parents, and without graduating from high school, married a man she barely knew. Roseanna, in turn, paid no mind to her daughter's accounts of their son-in-law abusing her. In fact, her husband and son-in-law became drinking partners and business associates. In the end, her daughter married three drinking, brawling men in succession, and by her last husband had a son.

   Roseanna reported that before her daughter started school, the two of them drove daily the twenty miles to her mother's home. She was going to show that she could take better care of her mother and daughter than her mother had done with her. She thrived on being indispensable to her mother and being "martyred" at home. When she eventually divorced, she sued her husband vindictively. Only her daughter's alienation, which cut her off from her grandson as well, finally heightened her consciousness.

   I couldn't "let go" until letting go was long overdue—let go of my drinking, of an abusive marriage, the grudges I have toward my mother, and the guilt for neglecting my daughter. I can see now that these memories were all too much for me, and I've already contacted a local counseling agency for help in my relationships with my mother and daughter.

   There is so much to do, and even more to undo, that I hope my life can unfold from this metaphysical self we all share. For our meeting I read something Martin Buber wrote that has been very helpful to me. He urged people to consider that they are "unique in the world and that none like them ever lived, for had there ever before been someone like them, then they would not have needed to exist."[5] So, maybe I needed the history I have. Accepting it keeps me involved in others' lives and more fruitful in my own. What comes of it all is still emerging.

Roseanna finds in the paradox of Engaged Detachment the insight that the embattled, forlorn life she has led "needed to exist." So too did the lives of those who intersected with her own. They now form the springboard propelling her to act in her best interest, all the while allowing "what comes of it" to emerge.

Many reviewers report how the paradox of metaphysical self is realigning their daily life. Some discover that attending to the theme of appreciating gifts received has recast their diminished future as the latest extension of gift-being-proffered to them. "And I've already informed my face so it shows I'm truly interested in spending time with others, in being a granny figure for children who pass my house with their parent or au pair each school day, and in calling a few neighbors each evening to check on how they are doing." They are increasing their generativity and decreasing their expectations out of the outcomes.

Notes and Recommended Readings

INTRODUCTION

Notes

1. Faulkner, W. 1994. *Requiem for a Nun.* In Blotner, J. and Polk, N. (Eds.). *William Faulkner: Novels 1942–1954.* New York: Library of America. 588. From *Requiem for a Nun by William Faulkner*, published by Chatto & Windus. Reprinted by permission of The Random House Group Limited.
2. Tillich, P. 1948. *The shaking of the foundations.* New York: C. Scribner's Sons. 53.

CHAPTER ONE: REMINISCENCE AND LIFE REVIEW

Notes

1. Shelley, P. B. 1965. "To Mary." *Complete Works.* New York: Gordian Press. 70.
2. The content on reminiscence and life review is an expanded revision of Magee, J. 1988. *A professional's guide to older adults' life review: Releasing the peace within.* Lexington, MA: Lexington Books. Chapter One. Reprinted with permission of Rowman and Littlefield Publishing Group.

Recommended Readings

Birren, J., and Cochran, K. 2001. *Telling the stories of life through guided autobiography groups.* Baltimore, MD: Johns Hopkins University Press.

Cohen, G. 2005. *The mature mind.* New York: Basic Books.

Gibson, F. 2004. *The past in the present.* Baltimore, MD: Health Professions Press.

Haight, B., and Webster, J. (Eds.) 1995. *The art and science of reminiscing: Theory, research, methods, and applications.* Washington, D.C.: Taylor and Francis.

Kunz, J., and Soltys, F. (Eds.) 2007. *Transformational reminiscence.* New York: Springer Publishing Company.

Price, B. 1995. *Family memories: A guide to reminiscing.* Forest Knolls: Elder Books.

Rosenbluth, V. 1997. *Keeping family stories alive: Discovering and recording the stories and reflections of a lifetime.* Vancouver, Canada: Hartley and Marks.

CHAPTER TWO: SELF AS MATURATION

Notes

1. Holmes, O.W. "The Chambered Nautilus." 1914. In C. Eliot (Ed.) *English poetry III: From Tennyson to Whitman.* The Harvard Classics, Vol. XLII. New York: P.F. Collier and Son. 61.

2. Kohut, H. 1977. *The restoration of the self.* New York: International Universities Press. 310.

3. Birren, J., and Deutchman. D. 1991. *Guiding autobiography groups for older adults.* Baltimore: Johns Hopkins University Press. 10.

4. Kinston, W. 1983. A theoretical context for shame. *International Journal of Psychoanalysis,* Vol. 64, 220.

5. Napier, N. 1990. *Recreating your self: Help for adult children of dysfunctional families.* New York: W.W. Norton. 116.

6. Riker, J. 1991. *Human excellence and an ecological conception of the psyche.* Albany: State University of New York Press. 122.

7. Mann, D. 1994. *A simple theory of the self.* New York: W.W. Norton. 35.

8. Whitman, W. 1982. "Song of Myself." *Complete poetry and collected prose.* New York: New American Library. 27.

Recommended Readings

Bandura, A. 1997. *Self-efficacy: The exercise of control.* London: Worth Publishers.

Baumeister. R. and Vohs, K. 2007. *Handbook of self-regulation: Research, theory, and applications.* New York: The Guilford Press.

Deci, E. 1995. *Why we do what we do: Understanding self-motivation.* New York: Penguin Books.

Dweck, C. 2000. *Self-theories: Their role in motivation, personality, and development.* Philadelphia: Taylor and Francis.

Elliot, A. and Dweck, C. 2005. *Handbook of competence and motivation.* New York: The Guilford Press.

Nadelman, L. 2004. *Research manual in child development, second edition.* Baltimore: Lawrence Erlbaum Associates.
Stickle, F. 2006. *Adolescent psychology, fifth edition.* New York: McGraw-Hill.

CHAPTER THREE: SELF AS SCRIPT

Notes

1. Millay, E. St.V. 1956. "Renascence." In Millay, N. (Ed.) *Collected poems.* New York: Harper and Brothers. 13. Reprinted by permission of Edna St. Vincent Millay Society.
2. The content on the transmission of intergenerational family dynamics is an expanded revision of Magee, J. 1988. *A professional's guide to older adults' life review: Releasing the peace within.* Lexington, MA: Lexington Books. Chapter Two. Reprinted with permission of Rowman and Littlefield Publishing Group.
3. Barksdale, L. 1989. *Building self-esteem.* Idyllwild, CA: The Barksdale Foundation. 14.
4. Roman, M. and Raley, P. 1980. *The indelible family.* New York: Ransom, Wade. 182.

Recommended Readings

Bengtson, V. 2005. *Source book of family theory and research.* Thousand Oaks, CA: Sage.
Coleman, M. and Genong, L. 2004. *Handbook of contemporary families.* Thousand Oaks, CA: Sage.
Howey, N. and Samuels, E. 2000. *Out of the ordinary: Essays on growing up with gay, lesbian, and transgendered parents.* New York: St. Martin's Press.
Kingson, E., Cornman, J., and Hirshon, B. 1986. *Ties that bind: The interdependence of generations.* Cabin John, MD: Seven Locks Press.
Lamanna, M.A. and Riedmann, A. 2006. *Marriage and families.* Belmont, CA: Thomson/Wadsworth.
McGoldrick, M., Gerson, R., and Petry, S. 2008. *Genograms: Assessment and intervention.* New York: W.W. Norton and Company.
Roloff Family and Sumner, T. 2007. *Little family, big values: Lessons in love, respect, and understanding for families of any size.* New York: Fireside.
Vangelisti, A. 2004. *Handbook of family communication.* Mahwah, NJ: Lawrence Erlbaum Associates.
Wallerstein, J. and Blakeslee, S. 2004. *What about the kids? Raising your children before, during, and after divorce.* New York: Hyperion.

CHAPTER FOUR: SELF AS METAPHYSICAL

Notes

1. Meng Tzu. 1970. *The Book of Mencius.* New York: Viking Penguin. 35.
2. Fakhruddin Iraqi. 1982. *Divine flashes.* New York: Paulist Press. 85. From the series by Paulist Press, *Classics of Western Spirituality.*
3. Walker, A. 1997. *Anything we love can be saved.* New York: Random House. 24.
4. Merton, T. 1966. *Conjectures of a guilty bystander.* New York: Doubleday. 180.
5. This section is an expanded revision of Magee, J. 2007. Life review, paradox, and self-esteem, in Doka, K. (Ed.) *Living with grief: Before and after the death.* Washington, D.C: Hospice Foundation of America. Chapter 2. Reprinted with permission of the Hospice Foundation of America.
6. Abd Allah Ansari. 1978. *Intimate conversations.* New York: Paulist Press. 63. From the series by Paulist Press, *Classics of Western Spirituality.*
7. Ibn Al'Arabi. 1980. *The bezels of wisdom.* New York: Paulist Press. 88. From the series by Paulist Press, *Classics of Western Spirituality.*
8. Fakhruddin Iraqi, *Ibid., 72.*
9. Maggid of Mezhirech. 1993. In Uffenheimer, R. (Ed.) *Hasidism as mysticism.* Princeton: Princeton University Press. 74.
10. Radha, S. 1981. *Kundalini: Yoga for the west.* London: Shambhala. 72.
11. Meister Echart. 1986. "Blessed are the poor." In McGinn, B. (Ed.), *Meister Echart: Teacher and Preacher.* New York: Paulist Press. 167. From the series by Paulist Press, *Classics of Western Spirituality.*
12. Julian of Norwich. 1978. *Showings.* New York: Paulist Press. 78. From the series by Paulist Press, *Classics of Western Spirituality.*
13. Meister Eckhart. 1986. "German Sermon No. 59." In McGinn, B. (Ed.) *Meister Eckhart: Teacher and Preacher.* New York: Paulist Press. 309. From the series by Paulist Press, *Classics of Western Spirituality.*

Recommended Readings

Aitken, R. and Steindl, D. 1996. *The ground we share.* Boston: Shambhala. 43.

Chakrabarti, C. and Haist, G. 2008. *Revisiting mysticism.* Newcastle, U.K.: Cambridge Scholars Publications.

Coward, H. 2002. *Yoga and psychology: Language, memory, and mysticism.* Albany: State University of New York Press.

Davis, A. and Dunn-Mascetti, M. 1997. *Judaic mysticism.* New York: Hyperion.
Mason, H. 1995. *Al-Hallaj.* Surrey, U.K.: Curzon Press.
Soltes, O. 2008. *Mysticism in Judaism, Christianity, and Islam: Searching for oneness.* Lanham, MD: Rowman and Littlefield Publishers.
Wiseman, J. 2006. *Spirituality and mysticism: A global view.* Maryknoll, NY: Orbis Books.

CHAPTER FIVE: SELF-ESTEEM

Notes

1. Shelley, P.B. 1965. "Ode to the West Wind." *Complete works.* New York: Gordian Press. 58.
2. Branden, N. 1987. *How to raise your self-esteem.* New York: Bantam Books. 26.
3. Nichols, M. 1991. *No place to hide: Facing shame so we can find self-respect.* New York: Simon and Schuster. 263.
4. Satir, V. 1988. *The new people making.* Mountain View, CA: Science and Behavior Books. 22.
5. California Task Force to Promote Self-esteem and Personal and Social Responsibility. 1990. *Toward a state of esteem.* Sacramento: California State Department of Education. 20.
6. Jacoby, M. 1990. *Individuation and narcissism: The psychology of the self in Jung and Kohut.* London: Routledge. 74.
7. Frey, D., and Carlock, C. J. 1989. *Enhancing self esteem.* Muncie, Indiana: Accelerated Development. 16.
8. Borba, M. 1989. *Esteem builders.* Rolling Hills Estates, CA: Jalmar Press. xix.
9. Nichols, *Ibid.*
10. Frey and Carlock, *Ibid.*, 120.
11. Gibran, K. 1980. *The prophet.* London: Heinemann. 36.

Recommended Readings

Dolan, S. 2006. *Stress, self esteem, health, and work.* Basingstoke: Palgrave Macmillan.
Healey, J. 2006. *Self esteem.* Rozele, N.S.W.: Spinney Press.
Kermis, M. 2006. *Self esteem: Issues and answers.* Hove: Psychology.
Kimeron, H. 2008. *Loving ourselves: The gay and lesbian guide to self-esteem.* Los Angeles: Turnaround.
Lindenfield, G. 2000. *Self esteem.* London: Thorsons.
Mruk. C. 2006. *Self-esteem research, theory, and practice: Toward a positive psychology of self-esteem.* New York: Springer Publications.
Owens, T., Stryker, S., and Goodman, N. 2006. *Extending self-esteem research: Sociological and psychological currents.* Cambridge: Cambridge University Press.
Preston, A., Hibbert, A., and Hesford, C. 2005. *Self esteem.* Blackburn: Eprint.
Thompson, L. 2009. *Self esteem: A manual for mentors.* Abergele: Studymates.

CHAPTER SIX: EMBEDDED SHAME

Notes

1. Joyce, J. 1991. *Dubliners.* New York: Penguin. 108.
2. Lewis, H.B. (1971). *Shame and guilt in neurosis.* New York: International Universities Press, p. 111.
3. Fogarty, T. 1977. Fusion. *The Family.* 4(2): 56.
4. Fossum, M. 1986. *Facing shame.* New York: W. W. Norton. 8.
5. Pipes, R., and Davenport, D. 1990. *Introduction to psychotherapy: Common clinical wisdom.* Englewood Cliffs, NJ: Prentice Hall. 249.
6. Satir, V. 1988. *The new people making.* Mountain View, CA: Science and Behavior Books. 67.
7. Sartre, J.-P. 1956. *Being and nothingness: An essay on phenomenology.* New York: The Philosophical Library. 62
8. Campbell, J., and Lavallee, L. 1993. *Who am I? The role of self-conceptual confusion in understanding the behavior of people with low self-esteem.* In Baumeister, (Ed.), *Self-esteem: The puzzle of low self-regard.* New York: Plenum Press. 12.
9. Lewis, M. 1991. *Shame: The exposed self.* New York: The Free Press. 151.
10. Nathanson, D.L. 1987. *The many faces of shame.* New York: Guilford Press. 111.
11. Lowen, A. 1983. *Narcissism: Denial of the true self.* New York: Macmillan. 94.
12. Lewis, H.B. 1987. *The role of shame in symptom formation.* Mahwah, NJ: Lawrence Erlbaum Associates. 63.
13. Anthony, E.J. 1981. *Shame, guilt, and the feminine self in psychoanalysis.* In Tuttman, S., Kaye, C., and Zimmerman, M. (Eds.), *Object and self: A developmental approach.* New York: International Universities Press. 211.
14. Miller, A. 1981. *Prisoners of childhood.* New York: Basic Books. 66.
15. Bradshaw, J. 1988. *Healing the shame that binds you.* Deerfield Beach, FL: Health Communications. 53.
16. Bednar, R.L., Wells, M.G., and Peterson, S.R. 1989. *Self-esteem: Paradoxes and innovations in clinical theory and practice.* Washington, D.C.: American Psychological Association. 4.

Recommended Readings

Ahmed, E. 2001. *Shame management through reintegration.* Cambridge: Cambridge University Press.
Delaney, T. 2008. *Shameful behaviors.* Lanham, MD: University Press of America.

Elison, J. 2007. *The self under siege: Coping with shame, guilt, and humiliation.* Cedar City, Utah: Southern Utah University.

Hansen, B. 2006. *Shame and anger: The criticism connection.* Washington, D.C.: Change for Good Press.

Kauffman, J. 2010. *The shame of death, grief, and trauma.* New York: Brunner-Routledge.

Logan, W. and Reeves, K. 2009. *Places of pain and shame: Dealing with "difficult heritage."* New York: Routledge.

Mack, A. 2003. *Shame.* New York: New School of Social Research.

Mollon, P. 2002. *Shame and jealousy: The hidden turmoils.* London: Karnac.

Morgan, M. 2008. *On shame.* New York: Routledge.

Seidler, G. 2000. *In others' eyes: an analysis of shame.* Madison, CT: International Universities Press.

Thomas, H. 2006. *The shame response to rejection.* Sewickley, PA: Albanel.

CHAPTER SEVEN: PARADOX

Notes

1. Rilke, R. 1978. *When silence reigns: Selected prose.* New York: New Directions. 97.
2. Winters, M. 2009. *Paradoxology.* Maryknoll, NY: Orbis Books. 8.
3. Zohar, D. 1990. *The quantum self: Human nature and consciousness defined by the new physics.* New York: Quill/William Morrow. 25.
4. Ibid. 58.
5. cummings, e.e. "anyone lived in a pretty how town." In *Complete poems, 1904–1962.* Copyright 1940, 1968, 1991 by the trustees for the e.e. cummings Trust. Used by permission of Liveright Publishing Publishing Corporation. 73.
6. *Romeo and Juliet,* Act I, Scene 4; *Sonnet 119.*
7. Ellis, J. 1998. *American sphinx: The character of Thomas Jefferson.* New York: Vintage Books. 118.
8. Stendhal. 1986. *The red and the black.* New York: Bantam Books. 209.
9. Redman, A. 1959. *The wit and humor of Oscar Wilde.* New York: Dover Publications. 61.
10. Kenner, H. 1948. *Paradox in Chesterton.* London: Sheed and Ward. 27.
11. Masefield, J. 1913. *The word.* In *Salt-water poems and ballads.* New York: Macmillan. 55.

Recommended Readings

Elson, L. 2010. *Paradox lost: A cross-contextual definition of levels of abstraction.* Cresskill, NJ: Hampton Press.

Goetz, I. 2002. *Faith, humor, and paradox.* Westport, CT: Praeger.

Kvanvig, J. 2006. *The knowability paradox.* New York: Oxford University Press.

Marar, Z. 2003. *The happiness paradox.* London: Reaktion Books.
Moore, T. 2000. *Original self: Living with paradox and authenticity.* New York: HarperCollins.
Olin, D. 2003. *Paradox.* Montreal: McGill-Queen's University Press.
Williamson, D. 1991. *The intimacy paradox.* New York: Guilford Press.

CHAPTER EIGHT: POETIC PARADOX

Notes

1. Clifton, L. 1987. *The book of light.* In *The collected poems of Lucille Clifton.* Copyright by Lucille Clifton. Reprinted with the permission of The Permissions Company, Inc. on behalf of BOA Editions Ltd., www.boaeditions.org. 46.

2. The following anthologies are abundant sources for poetic paradoxes: Baldwin, C., and Paul, H.G. (Eds.) 1985. *English poems.* Great Neck, NY: Roth Publishers; Friebert, S., and Young, D. (Eds.) 1989. *Longman anthology of contemporary American poetry.* New York: Longman Press; Moramarco, F. (Ed.) 1998. *Containing multitudes: Poetry in the United States since 1950.* New York: Twayne Publishers; Nelson, C. (Ed.) 2000. *Anthology of modern American poetry.* New York: Oxford University Press; Nims, J.F. (Ed.) 1981. *The Harper anthology of poetry.* New York: Harper and Row; Ramazani, J., Ellman, R., and O'Clair. (Eds.) 2003. *The Norton anthology of modern and contemporary poetry, Volume 1, Modern poetry; Volume 2, Contemporary poetry.* New York: W.W. Norton; Williams, O. (Ed.) 1980. *Immortal poems of the English language.* New York: Washington Square Press.

3. Chapters 8, 9, and 11 are expanded Revisions of Magee, J. 2007. *Life review, paradox, and self-esteem,* in Doka, K. (Ed.) *Living with grief: Before and after the death.* Washington, D.C.: Hospice Foundation of America. Chapter 2. Used with permission of the Hospice Foundation of America.

4. Frye, N. (Ed.) 1953. *Selected poetry and prose of William Blake.* New York: Modern Library. 47.

5. Thompson, F. 1922. *The hound of heaven.* New York: Dodd, Mead, and Company. 18.

6. Johnson, J.W. 1970. "Lift every voice and sing." In *Lift every voice and sing: Words and Music* by James Weldon Johnson, illustrated by Mozelle Thompson. New York: Hawthorne Books, Inc. Used by permission of Dutton, a division of Penguin Group (USA) Inc. 34.

7. Wordsworth, W. 1950. "The Tables Turned." *Poetical works with introductions and notes.* New York: Oxford University Press. 168.

8. Frye, N., *Ibid.*, 61.
9. Rumbold, V. (Ed.) 2007. "The Dying Christian to His Soul." *The poems of Alexander Pope*. New York: Pearson/Longman. 89.
10. Shelley, P.B. 1965. "Ode to the West Wind." *Complete works.* New York: Gordian Press. 58.
11. Pierce, E.L. 1966. *White wake in the sea.* Evanston, IL: Self-published. 32.
12. Head, J. and Aldrich, T.B. 1862. *Jewels from the quarry of the mind.* Boston: Henry A. Young. 56.

Recommended Readings

Danvers, J. 2006. *Picturing mind: Paradox, indeterminacy and consciousness in art and poetry.* New York: Rodopi.
Platt, P. 2009. *Shakespeare and the culture of paradox.* Burlington, VT.: Ashgate.
Wren, G. 2001. *A most ingenious paradox: The art of Gilbert and Sullivan.* New York: Oxford University Press.

CHAPTER NINE: WORD PLAY AS PARADOX

Notes

1. Frye, N. (Ed.) 1953. *Selected poetry and prose of William Blake.* New York: Modern Library. 25.
2. "But not for Me" (from *Crazy Girl*). Music and lyrics by George Gershwin and Ira Gershwin. Copyright 1930 (Renewed): *WB Music Corporation.* Reprinted with permission of Alfred Publishing.
3. "Lorelei" (from *My Cousin in Milwaukee*). Music and lyrics by George Gershwin and Ira Gershwin. Copyright 1932 (Renewed): WB Music Corporation. Reprinted with permission of Alfred Publishing.
4. "Together Wherever We Go" (from *Gypsy*). Lyrics by Stephen Sondheim and music by Jule Stein. Copyright 1959 (Renewed): Stratford Music Corporation and Williamson Music Co. All rights administered by Chappell and Company, Inc. Reprinted with permission of Alfred Publishing.
5. Simon, P. and Garfunkel, A. 1970. *Bridge Over Troubled Water.* New York: MetroLyrics.
6. The following resources were especially helpful: Hobbs, J.B. 1986. *Homophones and homographs.* Jefferson, NC: McFarland and Company; Kilpatrick, J.J. 1985. *The ear is human.* New York: Andrews, McMeel, and Parker; Linfield, J. 1993. *Word traps: A dictionary of 7,000 most confusing sound-alike and look-alike words.* New York: Macmillan.

7. Fry, C. 1985. "The Lady's Not for Burning." *Selected plays.* New York: Oxford University Press. Reprinted by permission of the Fry Estate.
8. Thorn-Drury, G. (Ed.) 1893. "Old Age." *The poems of Edmund Waller.* New York: Greenwood Press. 52.
9. Kern, J. and Hammerstein II, O. 1927. *Showboat.* New York: Hal Leonard.

Recommended Readings: Metaphors

Barker, P. 1985. *Using metaphors in psychotherapy.* New York: Brunner/Mazel.

Gibbs, R. (Ed.) 2008. *Cambridge handbook of metaphor and thought.* New York: Cambridge University Press.

Korecses, Z. 2010. *Metaphor: A practical introduction,* 2nd Ed. New York: Oxford University Press.

Lakoff, G. and Johnson, M. 1980. *Metaphors we live by.* 1980. Chicago: University of Chicago Press.

MacCormac, E.R. 1985. *A cognitive theory of metaphor.* Cambridge: M.I.T. Press.

Mills, J.C., and Crowley, R.J. 1986. *Therapeutic metaphors for children and the child within.* New York: Brunner/Mazel.

Sommer, E. 2001. *Metaphors dictionary.* Canton, MI.: Visible Ink Press.

Sontag, S. 2001. *Illness as metaphor and AIDS and its* metaphors. New York: Picador Press.

Recommended Readings: Homonyms

Knoblock, K. and Yates, R. 2001. *Synonyms, autonyms, homonyms.* Duncanville, TX: Bryan House Publications.

Michelson, R. 2002. *Dictionary of homonyms.* Dehli: IVY Publishing House.

Rayevsky, K. and Rayevsky, R. 2006. *Antonyms, synonyms, and homonyms.* New York: Holiday House.

Rothwell, D. 2007. *The Wordsworth dictionary of homonyms.* Ware, U.K.: Wordsworth Reference.

CHAPTER TEN: INTERGENERATIONAL PARADOX

Note

1. Goffman, E. 1974. *Frame analysis.* New York: Harper and Row. 210.

Recommended Readings

Burns, K. 2005. *Gay and lesbian families.* Farmington Hills, MI: Greenhaven Press.

Crouter, A. and Booth, A. 2003. *Children's influence on family dynamics: The neglected side of family relationships.* Mahwah, NJ: Lawrence Erlbaum Associates.

Meeker, M. 2006. *Strong fathers, strong daughters.* Washington, D.C.: Regnery Publishing.

Salmon, C. and Shackelford, T. 2008. *Family relationships: An evolutionary perspective.* New York: Oxford University Press.

Tannen, D. 2001. *I only say this because I love you: How the way we talk can make or break family relationships throughout our lives.* New York: Random House.

CHAPTER ELEVEN: THE PARADOX OF METAPHYSICAL SELF

Notes

1. Abbott, E. 1875. "The Dying Christian to His Soul." *A concordance to the works of Alexander Pope.* London: Chapman and Hall. 122.
2. Wolters, C. 1961. *Cloud of unknowing.* Baltimore: Penguin. 53–54. Copyright © Clifton Wolters, 1961, 1978. Reproduced by permission of Penguin Books Ltd.
3. Kook, A. 1978. *The lights of penitence; The moral principles; The lights of holiness.* New York: Paulist Press. 163. From the series by Paulist Press, *Classics of Western Spirituality.*
4. Fakhruddin Iraqi. 1982. *Divine flashes.* New York: Paulist Press. 114. From the Series by Paulist Press, *Classics of Western Spirituality.*
5. Buber, M. 1958. *Hasidism and modern man.* New York: Horizon. 111.

Recommended Readings

Duane, O. 1997. *Mysticism.* London: Brockhampton Press.
Eloir, R., Nave, Y., and Millman, N. 2007. *Jewish mysticism.* Oxford: Littman Library.
Heine, S. and Wright, D. 2004. *The Zen koan: Understanding classic texts.* New York: Oxford University Press.
Knysh, A. 2000. *Islamic mysticism: A short history.* Boston: Brill.
McGinn, B. 2006. *The essential writings of Christian mysticism.* New York: Modern Library.
Oliver, P. 2009. *Mysticism: A guide for the perplexed.* New York: Continuum.

Index

About the Author

Dr. James J. Magee is professor-emeritus of Counseling and Gerontology at The College of New Rochelle where he taught for 30 years. He was the inaugural chair and taught for seventeen years in the undergraduate Social Work department. For the next thirteen years he taught in the Counseling and Gerontology programs of the Graduate School.

His Social Work practice included family counseling both with Family Services of Nassau and in private practice. While teaching, he enrolled in the post-graduate training program in Family Therapy sponsored by the Center for Family Learning. He began conducting life review groups after specializing in Gerontology in the doctoral program at Fordham University's Graduate School of Social Service.

He is the author of *A Professional's Guide to Older Adults' Life Review: Releasing the Peace Within* and 40 articles and chapters on gerontological topics.

CPSIA information can be obtained at www.ICGtesting.com
Printed in the USA
BVOW032011201011

274085BV00002B/1/P